RUGBY LAW *explained*

2nd Edition

by Mike Mortimer

A DOWN TO EARTH GUIDE TO THE LAWS OF RUGBY UNION

Kairos Press
Newtown Linford
Leicestershire
1997

Second Edition
ISBN 1-871344-14-X

First published in 1996: ISBN 1-871344-07-7

Body text in Oranda BT 10pt.
Imagesetting by CDS Imaging, Leicester.
Cover design by Robin Stevenson, Kairos Press.
Cover pre-press by Cavalier Reproductions Ltd, Oadby, Leicester.
Printed in Great Britain by Norwood Press, Anstey, Leicester.

British Library Cataloguing in Publication Data
A catalogue record for this book is available from the British Library

Cover picture: Martin Johnson of Leicester Tigers vies with David Baldwin of Sale RFC in the 1997 Pilkington Cup Final.

Cover photograph & page 5 by Andrew Maw.

Cartoon illustrations by Tony Harding.

Additional illustrations by Roger Fairbrother.

Kairos Press
552 Bradgate Road
Newtown Linford
Leicester LE6 0HB

CONTENTS

FOREWORD TO THE FIRST EDITION BY DEAN RICHARDS OF LEICESTER TIGERS & ENGLAND

When asked by Mike Mortimer to write a foreword for his book, 'Rugby Law Explained', I had little hesitation for two reasons. In the first instance, all of these articles were written by Mike for the Leicester Tigers Official Programmes, over the 1994/95 and 1995/96 seasons. I, like all of the players, am very proud of our club programme, and are grateful to the team of contributors, under the editorship of Stuart Farmer, for the way they produce such a quality product. We are particularly proud now, as it has been declared 'Club Programme of the Year' for 1995/96. This award was made following a survey throughout the UK by the Rugby Memorabilia Society, who in their report wrote, "We were terribly impressed with the Leicester programme as it was near perfect". Thanks and congratulations are due to the editor, contributors, and the whole production team.

Secondly, I along with many of the players, have regularly read Mike's articles and have picked up one or two interesting little snippets of information that we otherwise would not have known.

I would not claim to be a studier of the Laws of the game, but I believe that any player, or indeed captain, wishing to maximise his effectiveness on the field-of-play, needs to have a very good understanding. I have also found it most beneficial to find out which laws the referees have recently been instructed to enforce more strictly, or apply differently. Knowing the latest interpretation is vital, especially in situations such as the tackle for instance, where the RFU instructions to the referees changed three times within the last season. Knowing what the referees are expecting of the players, and so avoiding giving away those silly penalty points, is an obvious advantage when playing high profile league, cup, and international rugby.

This book has covered some of the most complex law situations in a way that is accurate and up-to-date, and can be easily understood even by those who have never played the game. This is probably due to Mike's unique background, being one of the very few people who has both played and refereed the game to a very high standard.

In the 70s Mike played over 100 games in the front row for Leicester, where I am told he spent much of his time experimenting on how to 'bend' the laws to suit his own uncompromising style of play. Then after a brief spell playing local rugby, he joined the Leicestershire Society of Referees in the 80s, where he rapidly rose through the ranks to command the respect of the players and clubs as a firm but fair arbiter of the Law. It is difficult to resist using the old adage, 'poacher turned game-keeper', when referring to Mike as a referee.

I found 'Rugby Law Explained' very interesting. It covers most aspects of the game, and can be used as a reference book, or for light easy reading.

I enjoyed reading it – I hope you do.

Dean Richards,
Leicester, 1996

FOREWORD TO THE SECOND EDITION BY MARTIN JOHNSON OF LEICESTER TIGERS AND ENGLAND, AND CAPTAIN OF THE 1997 BRITISH LIONS SOUTH AFRICAN TOUR

Shortly after my return from the Lions South African tour I was approached by Mike Mortimer who asked me if I would write a few lines as a foreword to the second edition of his book, "Rugby Law Explained". Like Dean Richards, who wrote the foreword for the first edition, I accepted with little hesitation, as I knew that Mike was an old Leicester player, a local referee and that the articles in the book had been written in the first instance, for the Leicester Club's award winning programmes.

It was no surprise to me when I was told that the first edition copies of Rugby Law Explained had all been sold during the course of the 1996/97 Season, because the book did plug a gap in the already small Rugby Union library. To my knowledge, there is no other book on the bookshelves that has the prime objective of explaining and simplifying the games complex laws for the spectators.

Only after I agreed to write this foreword did I realise that I had a slight problem, brought about by the fact that the new edition is written in the same mould as the First Edition and Dean had made all of the most relevant points in his foreword. All I can really do is to endorse the salient points that were made by Dean, about how easy the book is to read and understand, and then highlight the difference between the two.

The Second Edition contains 16 additional articles, which when added to the re-writes gives a total of 48 topics. They are all up to date according to the laws as they stand for the beginning of the 1997/98 season and between them they cover the basics of every law in the official law book. The more complex subjects are supported by detailed illustrations and there is a sprinkling of 21 cartoons (11 new) which all go towards making an informative book, easy reading.

As the book is a compilation of Leicester programme articles accumulated over three seasons, it naturally comes in a series of short chapters, which for me gives the book it's most attractive feature. Each individual chapter deals with a particular subject in detail, but they are grouped together in such a way that they logically lead on one from another. In this way the book can be treated as light reading and read from front cover to the back, or it can also be used just as well for reference to clarify individual points of law.

I found the chapters on "The Officials" most interesting and enlightening. Having always been a player and on the receiving end of the referee's whistle, I have to confess that I had not previously given much thought to such things as "Referee Positioning – Referee Decision Making – Referee Training and Development". In fact there have been moments during games when I have been convinced that the referees themselves had not given much thought to the same. However, it is comforting to read that there is a structure to referee training and that they do consider such things.

In conclusion, I can say that I found the Second Edition of Rugby Law Explained very informative, easy to understand and in places quite amusing. I believe that it is ideal for all rugby enthusiasts who find themselves asking the question, "why did the whistle blow then?"

I am sure that this book will also be a "sell-out" just as its predecessor was.

Martin Johnson,
Leicester, 1997

THE TRY

The main objective of playing rugby football is to gain more points than the opposing team, by scoring drop-goals, penalty goals, tries and conversions.

drop-goals and penalty goals carry a value of 3 points, a conversion 2 points and a try is worth 5 points. There will be those amongst you who can remember the days when a try was only worth 3 points. It has been revalued upwards twice during my playing days, with the intention of encouraging teams to play a more positive passing and running game resulting in the scoring of more tries.

An on-side player can score a try by carrying or kicking the ball over the opponent's goal-line into the in-goal area and then being the first player to touch it down. Touching down requires the player to place downward pressure onto the grounded ball with the hands, arms or upper body (from waist to neck inclusive). The ball should be under the control of the player carrying it, or lying on the ground at the time it is touched down. The pressure applied must be downward and therefore if the ball, while lying in the in-goal area, is picked up by any player, this would not constitute a touchdown and the game should continue.

The goal-line is in the in-goal area and therefore a try should be awarded if the attacking player places downward pressure on the ball whilst it is on the line. The goal posts, which are set into the goal line, are also in the in-goal area and a try should be awarded if the ball is touched down while it is in contact with the ground and the base of the post. (I never thought that I would, but early in 1997 I had occasion to award such a try in a junior game at Lutterworth – A first for me!)

The corner posts, however, are in touch in-goal and therefore if one is touched by the ball carrier, before he is able to ground the ball in the in-goal area, a try should not be awarded. This would in fact be touch-in-goal and the game would be restarted with a 22 metre drop-out to the defending side.

If a ball carrier is tackled and the momentum of the player carries him into the opponents in-goal and he then touches the ball down, a try should be awarded. What one cannot do, is to propel the body further forward in order to reach the line, by using the arms or legs in a second action. However a player who has been tackled short of the line, but is in such a position that he is able to ground the ball on or over the line, without propelling his body forward a second time, should be allowed to do so. Provided a try is scored by the second placement of the ball this is legal. This is an exception to the very strict tackle laws and a further exception is that this is the only time that a tackler can legally try to stop the tackled player playing the ball. Although this law is quite clear, many senior referees do not allow tries to be scored in this way.

When there is doubt as to which team first grounded the ball in the in-goal, a scrummage should be formed five metres from the goal-line opposite the place where the ball was grounded. This also applies when a player is held up in the in-goal area and unable to ground the ball. A penalty try is awarded on occasions when in the opinion of the referee a try would probably have been scored – or scored in a more favourable position, had it not been for foul play on the part of the opposition.

THE PENALTY TRY

A penalty try can be awarded by the referee, to a team who would probably have scored a try, had it not been for an act of foul play by the opposing side. On such occasions, the referee should award the try in the most favourable place, directly between the goal posts. This should also be done, if a try would probably have been scored in a more favourable position, had it not been for an act of foul play by the opposition.

Following the award of a penalty try, the conversion kick should be taken anywhere along a line, parallel to the touch lines, running back from the centre of the posts. The conversion attempt of a penalty try is covered by the same laws as any other conversion and the opponents are allowed to attempt to charge it down, once the kicker has offered to kick the ball. The penalty is the fact that the kick is taken from the most favourable place and therefore more likely to result in two additional points to the non-offending team.

PENALTY TRY FOR REPEATED INFRINGEMENT

During the 1995 Varsity match the referee, Mr Tony Spreadbury, awarded a penalty try to Cambridge for repeated infringement by Oxford, who were the defending side. This being the first such decision in a high profile game, it instigated quite a lot of debate, with many of the learned members of the press concluding that such a decision was not supported by the laws of the game. How wrong they were!

The law states that "a Penalty-try should be awarded if, but for foul play by the defending team, a try would probably have been scored." Foul play is covered by law 26 which states – "Foul play is any action by a player which is contrary to the letter and spirit of the game, and includes obstruction, unfair play, misconduct, dangerous play, unsporting behaviour, retaliation and REPEATED INFRINGEMENTS."

This section in law dealing with repeated infringements, is most commonly applied to scrum-halves and hookers, who either put the ball in the scrum, or throw it in at the lineout, not straight. Most referee societies would agree that three consecutive, wilful offences of the above, would constitute repeated infringement and a penalty kick would be awarded to the non-offending team.

The Varsity match was different, because Oxford, who were defending their own goal-line, were repeatedly standing in front of the off-side line and closing down the space that Cambridge should have had to work in. Most referees would play advantage and if non occurred then award another penalty kick, which must of course be five metres out from the goal-line. Tony Spreadbury warned Oxford of the possible consequences of wilfully standing off-side and so, when they repeated the infringement, he awarded a penalty try, because in his opinion had it not been for such foul play, Cambridge would probably have scored anyway.

With the introduction of league and cup football, there is far more pressure on the teams to win the game and as a result defending players often deliberately kill the ball, or stand off-side, in the knowledge that the penalty kick is only worth 3 points, compared to a possible 5, or 7 for a try. This practice becomes even more prevalent once the attacking team are within 5 metres of the goal-line, because any subsequent penalty kick can only be awarded 5 metres out from the goal-line.

In 1996 the Rugby Union became professional and the "spirit" of the game was further put to the test. Unfortunately, the early signs have not been too good, as the "professional foul", or deliberate repeated infringements, have flourished. The referees responded in the best way they knew how, by awarding penalty tries and as a result 26 penalty tries were awarded in the First Division compared to 8 in the previous season.

Penalty try awards have now become so common, that there are grounds to suspect that they are being contrived, as an easy option to gain 7 points. Such practice is equally outside of the "spirit" of the game, as the repeated infringements which they were at first used to prevent. How will the referees respond next season, as the stakes of professionalism escalate even higher?

KICK AT GOAL AFTER A TRY

In order to encourage the scoring of more tries, the law gives the successful team the opportunity of scoring an additional two points, making the try worth a total of seven points in all. To beat this, an opposing team relying on penalties, or drop-goals, would have to score three times. The additional two point bonus is awarded if a member of the try scorer's team is able to kick the ball over the opponent's cross bar and between the goal posts.

The kick must be taken from somewhere on a line through the place where the try was scored and parallel to the touch line. Providing the ball is kicked from this line, it can be as close, or far away from the goal-line as the kicker chooses. The further back he chooses to go, the wider the angle, but the longer the distance. The nearer he chooses to place the ball, the shorter distance he has to kick, but the closer he will be to the opponents who can try to charge it down.

The kick should be taken with the ball that was in play when the try was scored and by any member of the try-scoring team. The kicker may use a place kick, or a drop-kick. For a place kick an approved kicking tee, sand or another member of the kicker's team may be used to steady the ball. An interesting fact is that if another player is used as a placer of the ball, the ball must remain in contact with the ground at the time it is kicked. Hardly fair, when sand and modern approved kicking tees, stand the ball up at least two inches above the ground.

The opposition should all be behind their own goal-line until the kicker begins his run-up. Once the kicker offers to kick the ball, they are then allowed to run out in an attempt to charge the kick down. If the opposition charge prematurely and the kicker fails to convert the ball, the kick should be taken again and the offending team ordered not to charge. On occasions when the defending side charge prematurely and the kicker is successful, then that kick should be allowed to stand.

Although the defending team are allowed to charge the kick, once the kicker has offered to kick the ball, they are not allowed to shout as they do so. Any such attempt should be penalised as ungentlemanly conduct. If the kick is successful it should stand and if not, the kick should be taken again with no charge allowed. The defending team members should also, not touch the goal posts while a kick is in progress.

If when the ball is in position it then topples off the sand or tee, before the kicker moves to kick it, the kicker should ask the referee for permission to replace the ball. If this is done the referee will tell the defending team not to charge while the ball is replaced on the tee. However, if the ball topples off the tee after the kicker has started his run-up to kick, the charge should be allowed to continue. Quick witted players have been known to salvage the two points from such disastrous occasions by quickly picking up the ball and drop kicking the goal from the same place – a perfectly legal action as the law does not require the kicker to stipulate the type of kick he wishes to use and the drop kick is a listed option.

The kicker should not be permitted to be unreasonably slow in taking the kick at goal and a period of one minute between the indication to kick and the actual kick is stated as being well within the zone of 'undue delay'. A player who is unreasonably slow should be warned and if he persists the kick should be disallowed and a kick-off ordered to the other team. Any time in excess of 40 seconds taken by the kicker should be added on to the time allowed for the same half, by the referee.

An experiment during the 1995/96 season saw the introduction of appointed RFU timekeepers, who sat in the stand with a stop watch and klaxon for the sole purpose of controlling the 40 minutes of playing time in each half. The appointments did not continue for the 1996/97 season and although there was talk of each club providing their own timekeeper, nothing has materialised to date. (see Time Keeping on Page 71)

THE DROP-GOAL

A drop-goal is worth three points and can be scored by any player by kicking the ball over his opponents' cross-bar and between the goal posts.

As seen on many occasions at Leicester, when they had the likes of Dusty Hare, Jez Harris and Les Cusworth around, it can be used as an easy option to score points against a stubborn defence. If the team cannot carry the ball through the lines of defence to the in-goal, then such talented players are able to notch up the points by going over the top. Many close games have been won by a last minute drop-goal.

A successful drop-goal should be kicked from the field-of-play and clear the opponents' cross-bar between the posts, without touching the ground, or any player of the kicker's team. A goal is scored if the ball crosses the bar, even if it is blown backwards afterwards, or it has touched either the cross-bar or a goal post on its way over. From the referees point of view drop-goals can present positional problems, as they are often unexpected and the referee would need to be close to the posts to be sure of making the correct decision.

Players may attempt a drop-goal from any situation in general open play, but a successful attempt to score in this way following the award of a free kick would be disallowed. Once a free kick has been awarded, that team are unable to score by way of a drop-goal, until after the ball next becomes dead, or the ball has been played, or touched by an opposing player. This restriction applies similarly, even if a team elect to scrummage, rather than take the free kick. This ruling was introduced in 1995, because too many teams included drop-goal specialist, like the three mentioned above, who were prolific points scorers from free kick situations. They were finding the target with monotonous regularity, while their opponents were forced to stand and watch helplessly, ten metres away.

It is my believe that the RFU were right to restrict the scoring opportunities of the drop-goal specialists and if I had my way, I would do away with them altogether. Although I concede that kicking skills have an important place in the game of rugby football, I would prefer to see them restricted to:– the kicking of penalties to punish foul play, or off-side; the gaining of territory by kicking for touch; and putting the opposition under pressure with up-and-unders.

The most memorable and enjoyable drop-goal for me was in fact a failed attempt, back in the 1970's, when I was playing for Leicester. My mate Ray Needham (presently the clubs Youth team manager and a committee man) was playing at loose head prop and while struggling across the field trying to get to a ruck in the opponent's twenty two area, found himself in the fly half position as the ball was emerging. John Allen who was playing at scrumhalf instinctively threw out the perfect pass, to the place where he expected to find his fly half, only to find Ray. So there was Ray, ball in hand, in an unfamiliar position on the opponents twenty two metre line. What would he do? You guessed! He attempted a drop-goal. The memorable thing about this attempt, was that Ray stubbed his toe, and had to go off.

Perhaps rather than ban drop-goals altogether, we could rule that they should be taken by front row forwards only, with a view to increasing the entertainments value of the game.

PENALTY KICKS

The loudest blow on the whistle of the referee usually indicates that he is about to award a penalty kick. Having blown his whistle in this way he should then indicate which side has been awarded the kick, by raising a straight arm, at an angle of 60 degrees to the horizontal, pointing in the direction of the non-offending side. (see Referee Signals, page 68) He should then indicate the mark from which the kick is to be taken, followed by a signal to show the reason for the penalty being awarded. On some occasions there may be a choice of two marks and then it is up to the captain of the non-offending side to choose which he prefers. For instance, if a kicker is obstructed after the ball has been kicked, the mark for the penalty could be where the obstruction took place, or where the ball comes to ground.

For penalty kicks that are awarded for offences committed when the ball is dead, the referee should make a mark where the ball would next have been in play, under normal circumstances. For instance if one hooker prevented his opposite number from throwing the ball in quickly by obstructing him, the referee should award a penalty to the non-offending side, fifteen metres in on the line-of-touch. When awarded a penalty the non-offending side always have the option of taking a scrummage at the mark instead of a kick.

Having elected to kick the penalty, it can be taken by any member of the non-offending team and by any form of kick with the following provisos:

- If the kicker chooses to hold the ball he must propel the ball out of his hands.
- If the ball is to be placed on the ground the kicker must propel it a visible distance. For this type of "tap kick" the kicker may keep his hand on the ball while he kicks it.
- If the kicker elects to kick for touch, the kick must be a punt, or a drop kick.

The kick should be taken within a one metre channel, on, or behind the mark, but not in front of it. A kick taken from the wrong place should be declared void and a scrummage awarded to the other side on the mark. The kick must be taken with the ball that was in play at the time the penalty was awarded, unless the referee decides that the ball is defective. Sand, sawdust or approved kicking tees are legally available for the kicker to place the ball on.

The kicker may play the ball in any direction and he can play the ball again, without any restriction, unless he has indicated his intention to kick at goal. Any indication of intention to kick for goal is irrevocable. If the kicker is taking a kick at goal, all players of the opposing team must keep still from the time the kicker commences his run until after the ball has been kicked.

When the penalty offence is within 5 metres of a goal-line the referee should always award the kick five metres out, on a line through the mark. A penalty kick should never be awarded closer than five metres from the goal-line. (International referees please note! – Ireland v England January 1995)

Players on the side who have been awarded a penalty should be behind the kicker when the ball is kicked and players of the other side should retire ten metres, or to their goal-line to avoid being offside. However, if their failure to be on-side is due to the speed at which the penalty kick was taken, then play should be allowed to continue.

TAP PENALTIES

Once a penalty, or free kick has been awarded, all players of the offending side should retire ten metres from the place where the referee makes the mark. Those who do not make it at the time the penalty kick is taken are off-side and therefore out of the game. They should continue to retire until they reach a distance of ten metres from the mark, unless they are played on-side.

In previous seasons, such off-side defending players were played on-side once the player taking the tap penalty had run five metres. This is no longer the case, as the law was changed in 1996. Now no action of the team taking the penalty will put defending players within the ten metre area on-side. However a player of their own side, who was back ten metres at the time the tap penalty was kicked, and therefore on-side, can advance as soon as the ball is kicked. At the time this player tackles the ball carrier, all other players in the defending team are then played on-side. Well coached teams will work hard at getting on-side defenders moving forward in such situations, as it will close down the space their opponents have to work in, and get their own off-side players back in the game more quickly.

In the past, quickly taken tap penalties were often ruled void by the referee because the kick had not been taken from the correct place. At that time the kick should have been taken from the mark indicated by the referee, or directly behind it. With a view to encouraging teams to run the ball and keep the game alive, the law has been changed allowing the kick to be taken in a one metre channel on either side of the mark. This gives the non-offending players a high degree of tolerance and the instances of tap-penalties being judged void has been greatly reduced.

Unfortunately many referees have been so keen to enter into the spirit of this new law, that they are now allowing kicks to be taken in front of the mark. This is unfair to the defending team, because they concede the stolen metres and more importantly loose the time that their opponents would have taken getting the ball back to the correct position, behind the mark.

At the same time the law was also changed, making it illegal for a team to organise what is commonly known as a cavalry charge within ten metres of their opponent's goal line. A cavalry charge is when the player who is about to take the penalty places the ball on the mark, while six or seven or even more players form up in a line across the field, some ten metres behind. On a given signal the players in this line charge forward, only when they are within two metres of the mark is the ball then kicked and passed to one of the oncoming players. The law makers believe that such a ploy is dangerous when carried out within 10 metres of the goal line, because the defending players who have to stand on the goal line until the ball is kicked, do not have enough space in which to get up the momentum required to make the necessary tackle. The team taking the tap-penalty always have the option of moving back the position from which they take such a kick, so that they are more than ten metres from their opponent's goal line, or alternatively the could transfer the ball through a second player's hands and run the cavalry charge off him. Both of these alternatives are within the law.

REFEREE CONTROL OF TAP PENALTIES

The laws relating to where and when a tap penalty might be taken were greatly relaxed at the beginning of the 1996/97 season. No longer was it necessary to ensure that all players on your own team were on-side, nor did the ball have to be kicked at, or behind the mark, it could be taken up to a metre on either side of the mark. Games have become more fluid, but new problems have been created for the referees.

Now, once a penalty, or free kick is awarded, alert scrumhalves (and most of them are) get the game started again immediately. When this is done, there is often no pattern to where the players of each team are positioned and it becomes extremely difficult to judge off-side decisions. Also, because of the quickness of the scrum-halves, the tap kick itself is often not seen by the referee.

On occasions when the team not in possession are penalised for not retiring the full ten metres (as they frequently are) the refereeing situation becomes even more difficult – bordering on impossible. As all coaches and players are fully aware that big advantages can be gained from such confusion, they have become a frequent tactic.

In order to create a manageable situation the referees have been asked to take their time when making the second mark. Until this mark is made, the non-offending players would not know where to take the kick and therefore he is able to legitimately slow things down, giving the offending team a chance to get ten metres back and on-side. This would appear to be a sensible idea, but is very dependant on the interpretation of the individual referee.

KICK-OFFS

The game starts with a kick-off at the beginning of each half and at resumption of play, following a score. The kick should be taken from the centre of the halfway line, although most referees will allow it to be taken a yard or two, to one side or the other, in order to find firm ground, or preserve the pitch.

The first kick of each half must be a place kick. The team that gets the right to take the first kick-off, or receive, is decided by the toss of a coin before the game starts. When the game re-starts following a score, a drop kick must be used. This kick should be taken at or behind the centre of the half way line, by the non-scoring team.

For all kick-offs, the players on the kicker's side must remain behind the ball until it has been kicked. Players should be particularly careful in the case of a drop-kick, as the kicker may choose to kick from a distance behind the actual half-way line. Failure to keep behind the ball until it has been kicked would result in a scrummage on the half-way line, with the put-in going to the non-offending team.

All types of kick-off must reach the line which is ten metres ahead of the half-way line, unless first played by an opponent. The players waiting to receive a kick-off should be behind the ten metre line until the ball has been kicked. If they move into this ten metre area after the ball has been kicked and then play the ball, they must accept all of the consequences and the game should continue.

On occasions when the ball does not reach the ten metre line and is not played by an opponent, the game will re-start with the kick taken again, or a scrummage to the receiving team, on the half-way line. The receiving team are asked to make the choice. If, when kicked off, the ball crosses the plane of the ten metre line and is then blown back by a strong wind, play should be allowed to continue.

On occasions when a kick-off is kicked directly into touch, without touching the ground or a player, the receiving team have the following options:

1) Accept the kick.
2) Have the kick-off re-taken.
3) Have the put-in at a scrummage, on the half-way line.

Option 1) is rarely taken, but if the kick was accepted, play would resume with a lineout, which would be back at the half-way line, because the kicker was not inside his 22 metre area and kicked directly into touch. I have not yet seen a team take a quick throw-in from this situation, which would be perfectly legal. In order to take a quick throw-in, the same ball as that kicked into touch must be used and it should only be handled by one player, who then throws it in so that it travels further than 5 metres at right angles to the touch line, at any point along the touch-line, behind the place where the normal lineout should be. The fact that this has not been done is probably just as well, as it would probably confuse everyone – referee included. When the ball from a kick-off crosses the opposing team's goal-line without touching or being touched by a player, the receiving team has the option of grounding the ball and making it dead, or playing on. If the ball is grounded and made dead the game would restart with another kick-off, or a scrummage on the halfway line.

For all kick-offs the ball must be kicked from the correct place and by the correct form of kick, otherwise it shall be kicked-off again – no advantage applies.

THE 22 METRE DROP-OUT

A drop-kick from behind the 22 metre line is a method used to restart the game, once the ball has crossed a goal line and there made dead. An attacking player might achieve this by kicking, or carrying the ball into touch-in-goal, or over the dead-ball line. The ball can also be made dead by a defending player touching the ball down in his own in-goal area, but a drop-out is only awarded providing the ball was carried, kicked, or charged down, over the goal line, by an attacking player. On occasions when the defending team take the ball into their own in-goal area and then are forced to touch it down, the attacking side gain the put in at a scrummage, five metres out from the goal line, level with where the ball was touched down.

When the defending side are awarded a drop-out, the kick can be taken from anywhere on, or behind, the twenty two metres line and by any player. As with all drop-kicks, the ball should be dropped from the hands and punted as it comes into contact with the ground. The ball must cross the twenty two metre line, otherwise the opposing team may have it dropped out again, or have a scrummage formed at the centre of the twenty two metre line. However, the advantage law does apply to this situation and if the opponents gain possession of the ball that is dropped out and does not cross the twenty two metre line, then play should continue. On occasions when the ball crosses the twenty two metre line and is then blown back, play should again be allowed to continue. If the ball is kicked directly into touch, the opposing team may accept the kick and take a lineout, have the ball dropped out again, or the put-in at a scrummage formed at the centre of the twenty two metre line.

Prior to the 1996 season, the kicker's team all had to be behind the kicker at the time the ball was dropped out. Now the law has changed and it allows the kick to be taken quickly, providing all the players who are in front of the kicker are retiring and continue to retire, until they are played on-side. The new ruling brings this law in line with the recently changed laws governing quickly taken penalties and free kicks. If the players were in front of the ball at the time it was kicked and not retiring, then the kick would be void, giving the opposing team a scrummage at the centre of the twenty two metre line. The attacking team, who are not taking the drop-out, should not charge over the twenty two metre line and if they do, the referee will ask for the kick to be re-taken.

A second change of law has now been introduced to deter players from deliberately kicking the ball dead behind their opponent's dead ball line, in the knowledge that they stood a fair chance of regaining possession from the resulting drop-out. This tactic was being used far too often, until the beginning of the 1996 season. Now when the attacking team kick the ball and it goes into touch-in-goal, or over the dead ball line, the defending team have the option of a drop out, or a scrummage. If they choose to scrummage, the mark for the scrum will be made at the place from where the ball was kicked. This is why the players have stopped using the boring tactic of deliberately kicking the ball dead from midfield positions and are running at the opposition. Another one the law makers have got right!

THE MARK, OR FAIR CATCH

Ask any fullback and he will confirm that having to wait under a ball that has been kicked skywards by an opponent, with eight burly forwards in chase, is a very un-nerving experience. In order to afford players in such a situation a little additional protection, the mark, or fair catch, was introduced to the laws of the game.

The mark is now very much a defensive play, as it can only be claimed from inside a player's twenty two metre area, or in his in-goal, which has not always been the case. When executed properly the referee blows his whistle as soon as the word "mark" is shouted and the ball is caught simultaneously. The player who called the mark is then awarded a free-kick on the mark.

Up until 1992, the player calling the mark had to be stationary, with both feet on the ground, cleanly catch the ball direct from a kick by an opponent, and at the same time shout "MARK!" This did require a little co-ordination and it was quite surprising how many claimed marks were not awarded, because the shout was not clear, or too late.

For the 1992/93 season the law was changed, doing away with the requirement for the player making the mark to be stationary, with both feet on the ground. From that date a fair catch could be awarded to a player who had at least one foot on the ground, cleanly caught the ball, and at the same time exclaimed "MARK!" This required a little less co-ordination and more importantly could be made by a player while he was on the move – remembering those marauding forwards.

In the 1996/97 season the law was changed yet again, stating that the player in his own 22 metres area only had to cleanly catch the ball and at the same time shout "MARK!" The requirement to have one foot on the ground was deleted and so it is now possible for a player who has jumped off the ground to make a mark. Should a player jumping for the ball land outside his 22 metre area, after catching the ball and shouting "MARK!" the mark should be awarded provided the ball was caught within the 22 metre area. The same ruling applies when a player lands in touch after catching the ball and shouting "MARK!" The mark should be awarded providing the ball was in the field of play at the time it was caught.

If the ball after being kicked by an attacking player, rebounds off a goal post, or cross bar, it can still be marked by a defending player, providing he complies with the other requirements of the law. Once a mark has been awarded, only the player who claimed it is allowed to take the resulting free-kick. If for some reason that player is unable to do so – maybe through injury – then the game would be restarted with a scrummage to the defending team at the place of the mark.

A little known but interesting fact, is that prior to 1992 a player could have claimed a "fair catch" from a ball that was knocked on, or thrown forward by an opponent. The removal of this option, so few years ago, has made very little difference, because even with my considerable years of playing and refereeing experience, I have never seen or heard of a player claiming a mark from a knock-on. I might also add, that even if a player did legally claim a mark in this way, the chances of the referee knowing that part of the law, were also pretty slim.

KNOCK-ON AND FORWARD PASS

A knock-on occurs when a player loses possession of, or propels the ball with his hands or arm, towards his opponents' dead ball line, which then touches the ground, or another player, before it is recovered by that player. If the ball is knocked forward one or more times by a player who is in the act of catching it, and he recoveres it before it has touched the ground or another player, then it is an adjustment and not a knock-on.

For an unintentional knock-on a scrummage will be awarded, usually at the place of infringement, with the put-in to the non-offending team. It is an offence to intentionally knock-on, and in 1992 the penalty for this was changed from a penalty-kick to a free-kick, which surprised many people. However sense prevailed, and this decision, which only lasted four years, was reversed for the 1996/97 season. The penalty for a deliberate knock-on is now a penalty kick to the non-offending side.

A knock-on can occur anywhere in the playing area, which includes the field of play, and the two in-goal areas. For a knock-on by either team that happens in an in-goal area, the referee should award the scrum to the non-offending side, in the field of play, five metres from the goal-line, and in line with the infringement.

As usual, the referee will look to see if the non-offending team can gain an advantage after a knock-on, but there is one occasion when such an advantage is not allowed. If an attacking player knocks the ball forward in the field of play and the ball travels into the in-goal area, where it is then grounded by a player, or goes into touch-in-goal, or over the dead-ball-line, a scrummage will be awarded at the place of the knock-on. This is done because the law makers believe that to allow the defending team to gain a 22 metre drop-out from this situation, simply by touching the ball down, is far too great an advantage, in view of the fact that their opponents were threatening to score a try.

A knock-on occurs, when the ball is propelled forward from a player's hands or arms. It is not a knock-on if the ball is headed forward (soccer style). This was a ploy that was regularly used by Robin Money, who played full-back for Leicester in the 1970s.

Any on-side player is allowed to pass the ball, or propel it with his hand, providing that it does not travel towards his opponent's goal-line. A flat pass, or a pass parallel to the goal-line, is therefore perfectly acceptable. If a pass is not thrown forward, but bounces forward after hitting the ground or another player, the referee should again allow play to continue.

When a player hands the ball to another player of his own team without any propulsion, or throwing of the ball, this also constitutes a pass. Therefore, if the receiving player is in front of the player handing him the ball the pass should be judged to be forward. A very strict referee might judge the receiving player to be off-side and award a penalty against him, instead of a scrummage for the forward pass.

It should be noted, that a player is allowed to knock the ball forward without penalty, when the ball is charged down from an opponent's kick. For this to be legal the player should make no attempt to catch the ball, but simply charge forward with his hands and arms outstretched, with a view to stopping the kick being made.

OFF-SIDE IN OPEN PLAY

This article attempts to simplify off-side when the ball is being passed, run with, or kicked by a player, in what is generally known as "Open Play". It does NOT apply to rucks, mauls, scrums, or lineouts, where the off-side laws are different.

In open play, a player is off-side if the ball has been kicked, deliberately touched, or is being carried by one of his own team behind him. The off-side line is an imaginary line drawn parallel to the goal lines, through the point where the ball was last played, or is being held by a player. All players on the same team, who are in front of this imaginary line, are off-side. Contrary to many people's understanding, off-side law applies from dead ball line to dead ball line and therefore a player can be off-side in his own in-goal area.

It is important to realise that being off-side in itself, is not a penalty offence, it simply means that you are out of the game. An off-side player should only be penalised if he plays the ball, obstructs an opponent, or moves towards an opponent waiting to play the ball, before he is put on-side.

An off-side player should be looking to get himself on-side and therefore back in the game. He can do this by running back behind the imaginary off-side line himself, or waiting for team mates to advance the off-side line. This can be done by the player who last played the ball, or any other player who was on-side at that time, running forward. The imaginary off-side line will advance at the rate of the fastest on-side player.

Off-side players can also be played on-side, by actions taken by their opponents. Once an opponent gathers the ball and runs five metres, kicks, or passes the ball, all players on the other side become on-side immediately, regardless of where they are standing in relationship to the ball.

However, it would not be rugby if we did not have an exception to the rule! When the ball is kicked forward up field, any off-side player who is within a 10 metre radius circle of an opponent waiting to play the ball, or of the place where the ball lands, should retire without delay and without interfering with an opponent. No action taken by an opponent will put a player within this circle on-side, and referees are advised to interpret this law strictly. Players are NOT allowed to stand still in this area, they must make the effort to get away.

Players and coaches are looking for strict refereeing of ALL off-side law, because the players who are allowed to encroach off-side are negative and unfairly stifle good, flowing, open rugby!

The RFU recognise that off-side has become prevalent and in view of the complexity of the laws, coupled with the increasing speed of players, it is now thought to be an impossible task for one official. For this reason, all referees officiating in division one games were 'wired up' with their touch judges, by two-way radio at the beginning of the 1996/97 season. This effectively added two extra pairs of eyes to the task of keeping the players on-side and giving the side in possession their legal space in which to work. Unfortunately this scheme was abandoned in its early days, as many of the referees found it to be counter productive, but they continue to work as a team of three with their touch judges, relying on hand signals. (see The Touch Judge, page 76)

OFF-SIDE AT RUCK & MAUL

As soon as a ruck, or maul, is formed during a game of rugby the off-side lines change immediately, for all players of both teams. For this reason, it is absolutely imperative that players, referees and those who wish to understand the game, know exactly what constitutes a ruck, or a maul.

In the simplest terms, a ruck is formed when the ball is on the ground and a minimum of two players (one from each side) are on their feet and bound together with the ball between them. This situation usually arises after a ball carrier has been tackled and the supporting player is grabbed by an opponent, before he has a chance to pick up the ball. Once the ruck is formed in this way, any on-side player can join, but the ball must only be played with the feet.

A maul is formed when the ball carrier is on his feet and held by a minimum of two players (one from each side). It is important to remember that there must be a player of the ball carrier's side involved. A ball carrier surrounded by four, or five opponents, might look like a maul, but is simply a joint attempt to tackle, or dispossess the ball carrier. As with a ruck, any on-side player can join a maul.

Following a ruck, or maul, all players on the side without possession, are put on-side, as soon as an opponent runs five metres with the ball, or kicks the ball, regardless of their position relative to the ball. Therefore in open play, when the ball is being run and passed between players, only those in the side in possession can be off-side. BUT, this changes with the formation of a ruck, or maul.

As soon as we have a ruck or a maul, two clear cut imaginary off-side lines are introduced immediately. These off-side lines run across the field, parallel to the goal lines, through the back foot of the hindmost player in each side of the ruck or maul. All players who are in front of the their respective off-side line, are themselves off-side, and cannot take part in the game, until they retire to an on-side position, behind the line.

Players wishing to join the ruck or maul, must approach from an on-side position and bind to the hindmost player of their own team. They cannot join on to the side of the ruck or maul, nor can they loosen their bind and slide down the sides. Players can leave a ruck or maul at any time, but if they do they must immediately retire to an on-side position.

All players who do not join the ruck or maul, must remain behind their respective off-side line at all times, until the ruck or maul is over. In the case of a maul, this often means that players have to retreat if their opponents get a drive on.

Rucks and mauls can only take place in the field of play and therefore, when the ball in a ruck or maul, is on or over, a goal line, the ruck or maul is over. This means that the ruck and maul off-side lines are no longer in operation and players should treat it as an open play situation.

Referees should be very strict and penalise any players who do not comply with these laws, because off-side players are putting a strangle hold on our game. Particular attention should be paid to:

- Players joining onto the side and not the hindmost man.
- Players loitering on the sides of rucks and mauls
- Players sliding down the sides with loose binding.
- Players not in the ruck or maul encroaching in front of the off-side line.

OFF-SIDE IN THE LINEOUT

When the ball goes into touch, the touch judge marks the place where the resulting throw-in is to take place, which should be where the ball broke the plane of the touchline. An imaginary line from this point, drawn across the field, parallel to the goal lines, is called "The line-of-touch". The lineout is formed by each team lining up half a metre on each side of this line.

There must be at least two players from each team in the lineout and the maximum number is determined by the side who have the right to throw the ball in. Besides the players that line up to form a lineout, both scrum halves, the player throwing the ball in and his opposite number, are all considered to be part of the lineout. The line-of-touch is the off-side line until the ball touches a player, or the ground. Once the ball has been caught, or it touches the ground, the off-side line runs through the ball itself. So the players taking part in the lineout should stay on their own side of the line-of-touch until the ball arrives, and then they should remain behind the ball until the lineout ends. However, a player who has jumped unsuccessfully for the ball and crossed the line-of-touch, should not be penalised if he retires immediately to an on-side position.

The player throwing the ball, should stand in touch while making the throw. Once the ball is thrown, he can then take up a position in the field of play, so long as he remains behind the line of touch, which is also his off-side line. The direct opponent of the player throwing the ball in, is the only other forward allowed to stand between the 5 metre line and the touch line, and he too must remain behind the line-of-touch. The other forwards who are forming the line should not take up a position beyond the 15 metre line, unless the ball is thrown directly to them, otherwise they would be off-side.

All players not taking part in the lineout (usually the three-quarters) must take up positions behind another imaginary line parallel to the goal lines, but 10 metres back from the line-of-touch. Should the lineout be awarded nearer than 10 metres to one team's goal-line, the goal-line itself becomes their off-side line. These players should not advance in front of the off-side line until the lineout is over.

So when is the lineout over? A very important question, because the off-side lines change dramatically, between the time one starts and the time it ends.

A lineout starts when the ball leaves the hands of the player throwing in, and it ends in one of the five following ways:

1) When the ball is passed, or tapped out of the lineout.
2) When a ball carrier runs out of the lineout.
3) When the ball travels beyond the 15 metre line.
4) When a ruck, or maul forms and the back feet of one team moves beyond the line-of-touch.
5) When the ball becomes unplayable and the referee blows the whistle.

Knowing the above law is very important, because while the lineout is still in progress the two sets of backs are usually at least 20 metres apart. It is probably the only time in the game that the backs are assured of this amount of space and time to work in. That is why the better coaches and players spend a lot of time developing the two handed catch in the lineout. When ball is secured in this way the lineout is not immediately over and the opposing backs are not allowed to advance.

The penalty for being off-side in a lineout is a penalty kick, and as they are always awarded at least 15 metres in from the touch line, they frequently result in a three point goal. When the threequarters are caught off-side, that penalty kick is at least 10 metres closer to the goal posts and therefore, even more kickable. So as the penalty for being off-side in the lineout, frequently results in points on the board for the opposition, one would think that the players would "brush-up" on the relevant laws. My experience is that very few of them are able to quote the five ways that a lineout can end and therefore they cannot be sure when it is safe for the threequarters to advance.

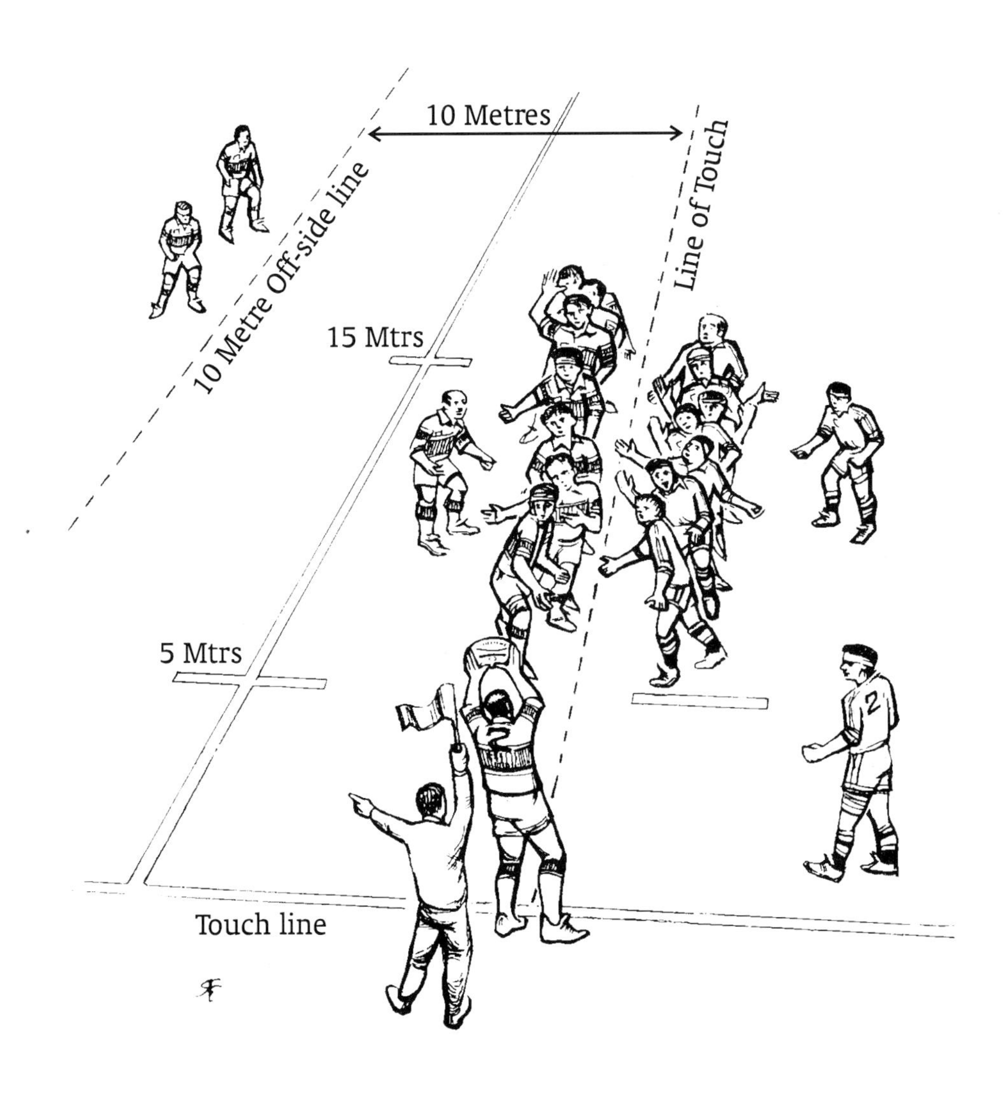

THE TACKLE

When play breaks down because the ball is out of play, or there has been an infringement of the law, the game is simply stopped and restarted with a line-out, drop-kick, or a scrummage. This is not the case when the breakdown is caused by a player being tackled. On such occasions the game is allowed to continue, in the hope that the ball will remain available for arriving players.

A tackle occurs when the player carrying the ball is held by an opponent and is brought to the ground, or the ball he is carrying comes into contact with the ground. He is deemed to have been brought to the ground, if he is on one knee, both knees, sitting on the field of play, or is on top of another player, who is on the ground. A ball carrier who is held by an opponent, but remains on his feet, is NOT tackled, NOR is he tackled if he has been knocked to the ground and is not being held.

Following a tackle, the ball carrier may take a number of options, but whichever one is chosen, it must be actioned immediately. The tackled player may pass the ball, release the ball, or get up and move away from the ball. The requirement to release the ball, allows the player to put the ball on the ground, or even to push it along the ground in any direction, except forward. The interpretation of "immediately" is very much at the discretion of the referee, but as they are all very keen to see the ball kept alive following a tackle, they tend to be quite lenient. This is particularly so, if the tackled player is moving the ball back and away from his body.

On the contrary, the player who executes the tackle, must do nothing which prevents the tackled player from playing the ball, and so keen are the RFU to keep the ball alive after a tackle, they amended the law yet again in 1996. Now any player who tackles an opponent and in doing so, goes to ground, must immediately release the tackled player and get up, or move away from the tackled player and the ball. He must not play the ball until he is on his feet. Previously the law did not make it clear that the tackler had an obligation to move away from the ball. Referees have now set priorities for the tackle situation and will look to penalise the tackler first, the ball carrier second and arriving players who do not stay on their feet third.

Once the ball has been played by the tackled player, none of the players on the ground, may interfere with the ball, or attempt to tackle an opponent who picks up the ball. In effect they are out of the game until they get back onto their feet. Players not involved in the tackle, may play the ball on arrival, providing they stay on their feet. If individuals, who are on the ground, have played according to the law, the ball should be available for the first player arriving to pick up. If it is not, then he must resist the temptation of going to ground, or he will be penalised. Alternatively, if he remains on his feet and the players on the ground prevent him from picking it up, it is they who will be penalised.

On occasions where players from both sides arrive at the same time, and they engage with the ball still on the ground between them, a ruck is deemed to have been formed.

It is very important that the referee applies the law strictly after a tackle and that the first offender is the one that is penalised. Often, potentially good games of rugby are ruined, because the ball is not recycled after the tackle, resulting in a pile-up of players and the inevitable scrummage or penalty. Referees should concentrate on the following points:

1) Ensure the tackler allows the ball carrier to play or release the ball.
2) Ensure that the tackler moves away from the ball and the tackled player.
3) Ensure that the tackled player passes, or places the ball away from his body immediately.
4) Ensure that the arriving players stay on their feet, and do not deliberately dive onto, or over the ball.
5) Be sure to penalise the FIRST offender!

Since the interpretation of the law changed and the referees began to penalise tackling players for not releasing the ball carrier and moving away, some players have developed new techniques. They have learnt how to tackle a player while remaining on their own feet all of the time, or on occasions when they have to go to ground, they use their momentum to roll straight back up on to their feet. In this way they are able to achieve the tackle, (putting their opponent out of the game and requiring him to release the ball) and at the same time keep themselves in the game. They are therefore able to play the ball as soon as it is released by the tackled player. Unfortunately this new skill, which has been mastered by Leicester's Neil Back as well as anyone, is so revolutionary, that some referees have not worked out what is happening yet and good positive play is being penalised.

THE RUCK

A ruck is formed when the ball is on the ground and one, or more players, from each team, while on their feet, are closing around it, in physical contact. This situation usually arises following a tackle, where the first supporting player fails to pick the ball up, before the arrival of an opponent. It is very important to know when the situation changes from a tackle to a ruck, because it affects what the players are allowed to do next.

In open play, there is no off-side for the team who do not have possession and a player from that team could approach the tackle situation from any direction and pick up the ball. For the team in possession, the ball is the off-side line and they should only approach it from their own side.

Once a ruck has been formed at the place of the tackle, the approaching players of both teams can only join on their own side of the ruck and the ball can only be played with the feet. The new off-side lines are imaginary lines which run parallel to the goal lines through the feet of the hindmost player in each side of the ruck. Players should only approach from behind the new off-side line, joining alongside, or behind the hindmost player. They should then bind on with the whole of one arm around the body of a team mate.

All players not wishing to join the ruck must retire to behind the off-side line and not loiter around the sides. Those who are in the ruck can leave at any time, providing they also immediately retire behind the off-side line. While in the ruck, all players should have their head and shoulders above their hips at all times and nobody should do anything that might cause the players in the ruck to collapse.

While the ball is in the ruck, the players should only play it with their feet and when rucking for the ball, they should step over players lying on the ground. Any such rucking should only take place in close proximity to the ball. Referees are instructed to deal very severely with players who wilfully trample on others lying on the ground and if a boot makes contact with a players head, it should always be regarded as intentional and dealt with accordingly.

On occasions when the ball becomes un-playable, the referee should stop the game and award a scrummage to the team who were going forward immediately prior to the formation of the ruck. Whilst the ball is in the ruck, the scrum-half, or the player standing in that position, must do nothing to convey to his opponents that the ball is out. This law was introduced in 1996 to bring the ruck in line with the law for scrummaging, where scrumhalves have not been allowed to dummy a pass for three years. This puts a stop to the practice of contriving penalties by luring an opponent off-side.

When players drive, or are driven to the ground, in the absence of opposition, the referee should recognise that no ruck has been formed and that this is not an infringement of the law.

The secret of good rucking is for the players to arrive at the breakdown early, in numbers, bound on to each other and then hit the area directly behind the ball, low and hard. The players should work hard to stay on their feet, so that they can maintain the drive. When this is done well, it will clear the opposition players and leave the ball for the scrumhalf to pick up.

RUCKING OR OBSTRUCTION?

The purpose of a ruck is to give both teams an opportunity to win possession of the ball, when it has been taken to the ground and open play has ended. While rucking players engage with their opponents close to the ball and they are all bound on to one another, this is good rugby, but unfortunately teams have been stretching the letter of the law to the limit and many unfair practices have been coached.

One such practice became known as 'Scatter Rucking'. Here instead of focusing at the point where the ball was put on the floor and binding onto one another, the players deliberately spread themselves over a wide area (some three or four metres on either side of the ball) and charge in with their arms outstretched. This charge continues past the point where the ball is on the floor, and consequently all the opposition players anywhere near the ball are swept to the side and those who are behind the ball cannot get to the point where the ruck should be taking place. I am sure that you will all recognise this practice for the blatant obstruction that it surely is.

Referees are now advised that players may go beyond the ball, providing they do not obstruct opponents in the actions they take (e.g. turning their backs to the opposition or 'scatter rucking' with arms outstretched). Rucking players may only engage with the opposition when in close proximity to the ball. They should attempt to step over players on the ground without contact and should be allowed to take one step before engagement. Any engagement with opponents after this second step would be considered to be obstruction by the referee.

THE MAUL

A maul is formed when a ballcarrier is on his feet and held by a player from each team. It therefore requires a minimum of three players to form a maul. However, it should be remembered, that a ballcarrier surrounded by two, or more opponents, does not constitute a maul, it is simply a multi-handed attempt to tackle. To become a maul, it must be joined by a member of the ball carrier's team.

It is very important to know when an attempted tackle becomes a maul, because it effects what the players are allowed to do next. Once a maul has been formed the approaching players of both teams, can only join on their own side of the maul. The new off-side lines are imaginary lines which run parallel to the goal lines, through the feet of the hindmost player in each side of the maul. Players should only approach from behind the new off-side line, joining alongside, or behind the hindmost player. They should then bind on with the whole of one arm, around the body of a team mate.

All players not wishing to join the maul must retire to behind the off-side line and they should not be allowed to loiter around the sides. Those who are in the maul can leave at any time, providing they also immediately retire behind the off-side line. While in the maul, all players should have their head and shoulders above their hips at all times and nobody should do anything that might cause the maul to collapse.

In the 1993/94 season the players could only bind onto the hindmost player on their side of the maul. This made it very easy for the referees to spot the players who were sliding down the sides of mauls, with a view to killing the ball, but it also created new problems. Players and coaches were quick to realise, that by moving the ball back to the last man in the maul, their opponents, who were not allowed down the sides, could never legally get anywhere near it. As a result we had the introduction of prolonged mauls, slowly trundling on towards the opponents goal-line and well drilled packs could keep this up indefinitely. Continuous rolling mauls, no matter how well executed, are not what the law makers intended and so amendments were made in the 1994/95 season.

The new law stated that when a maul becomes stationary, or the ball becomes unplayable, a scrum should be awarded to the side who were NOT in possession at the time the maul began. When a maul is stationary, the referees have been asked to say "use it or lose it!" – referring to the ball of course. The side in possession will then be given reasonable time for the ball to emerge, or else the whistle will be blown.

There is an exception made when a player catches the ball direct from a kick by an opponent (other than from a kick-off or a drop out) and is immediately held by an opponent so that a maul is formed, his team will put in the ball at the ensuing scrummage.

An interesting point to note is that the ruling for the ruck when the ball becomes unplayable is the opposite and the team who were moving forward immediately prior to the formation of the ruck get the put in at the resulting scrummage. Now, as it is legally possible to turn a maul into a ruck by simply placing the ball on the floor, or the ball carrier (on his own) going to ground, the better teams will do this when the maul begins to lose momentum in order to keep possession.

FROM RUCK TO MAUL

There is NO WAY in which a ruck can be changed into a maul legally. Quite surprising really, as the highest ranking referees allow it to happen week after week. I believe, that I saw it happen at every single first-class game that I attended in the 1996/97 season (including internationals) and never once was it penalised.

As the ball appears at the back of a ruck, it can be picked out by a player standing in the scrum-half position, providing he does not burrow in too far. This player then has the option of passing, kicking, or running with the ball. The referee will be reasonably sympathetic to the player reaching into the ruck for the ball, but once he places his hands on it, the ball is deemed to be out and the off-side lines change immediately. The ball can also be picked up by a player who is bound on at the back of a ruck, providing that he completely detaches himself from the ruck as soon as he has it in his hands. He then has the same options as the player standing in the conventional scrum-half position – he can pass, kick, or run with the ball.

What he cannot do, is to pick up the ball that is lying at his feet, while still maintaining upper body and shoulder contact with his own team mates and then, without ever having lost contact, tuck the ball under one arm and bind on again with his other arm, thus starting a rolling maul. When this happens the players of the same team as the ball carrier should be penalised for being off-side and obstructing, or else the ball carrier penalised for handling the ball in the ruck. Either way it should always result in a penalty kick to the non-offending side. This practice is most unfair and is becoming increasingly popular with the players, as it continues to go on unrecognised by the referees.

FORMING A SCRUMMAGE

The scrummage is the method used to restart a game of rugby following minor infringements, or if the referee decides that the ball is not playable. The team not responsible for the stoppage will be allowed to put the ball into the scrummage, which is an advantage, because they are able to choose the side of the scrummage they wish to put the ball in. The left hand side is usually selected, simply because the loosehead prop (who binds on the left hand side of his hooker) must have his head outside the head of the opposing tighthead prop and as heads from each side must alternate, this places the non offending team's hooker one body width nearer to the ball and he therefore should win the strike. The place for a scrummage is usually where the infringement, or stoppage occurred, unless that place is inside the in-goal area, or near to a goal-line, or a touch line. If in the in-goal area, the scrum should be formed five metres out from the goal-line opposite the place of the infringement, and if less than five metres from a touch line, brought in from the touch line to the inside of the five metre line. For infringements that happen close to a goal-line the scrummage should be formed so that all the feet of the defending team are in the field of play (that is, not in the in-goal area). In all instances, the scrum should be formed without any intentional delay.

Each front row must consist of no more and no less than three players and each team must pack with no more and no less than eight in total. There used to be no limit to the number of players that a team could play in the scrummage, others being allowed to join by binding along side the second row, or by forming a third, or even a fourth row. However, the law was changed in 1996, and now insists that the number of players bound into each pack is balanced, for safety reasons.

Before the two front rows engage they must be standing not more than an arm's length apart, all sixteen forwards in position and the ball should be in the hands of the scrum-half, ready to be put in. The front rows should then crouch, so that when they meet, each player's head and shoulders are no lower than his hips, and no player's head is next to the head of a team mate. Only when the referee is satisfied that everything is correct, will he then invite the two front rows to engage.

The scrummage will always be a priority aspect of the game in the eyes of coaches and players for the following reasons:

1) Scrummages provide the opportunity to win the ball
2) Props are forced into physical contact with their opponent every time a scrummage is awarded.
3) Scrummages are recurring and if there is a problem it is not simply going to go away.
4) Sixteen players are directly involved giving the referee plenty of potential problem areas to watch, besides the two scrumhalves and off-side in the backs.

Therefore it is absolutely essential that the referee sets his parameters clearly at the first scrummage and that the players know what is expected of them. If he can get the two front rows to engage and settle so that both sides believe they are getting a fair chance to compete for the ball, then he will be 90% towards gaining trouble free scrummaging.

If the two packs have engaged and the resulting scrummage is stable, a wise referee will leave it alone. (If it's not broke don't fix it). On the other hand, if it is unstable it means that one, or more, of the participants are unhappy and he should quickly re-check all of the binding and body positions of the players, paying particular attention to the front rows. The front row players are of prime importance, because they form the platform for all of the other players and if they are not set correctly things are bound to go wrong. Exactly what might go wrong and what the referee might do about it, is a complex subject dealt with in a later chapters. (see Who collapsed the scrummage? Page 36)

SIDE ELEVATION OF A SCRUMMAGE SHOWING GOOD BODY POSITIONING

1) Backs of all players are flat and parallel to the ground.
2) No player has his shoulders lower than his hips.
3) The binding is correct and no players are pulling downwards.
(Wing forwards are not shown in the diagram above)

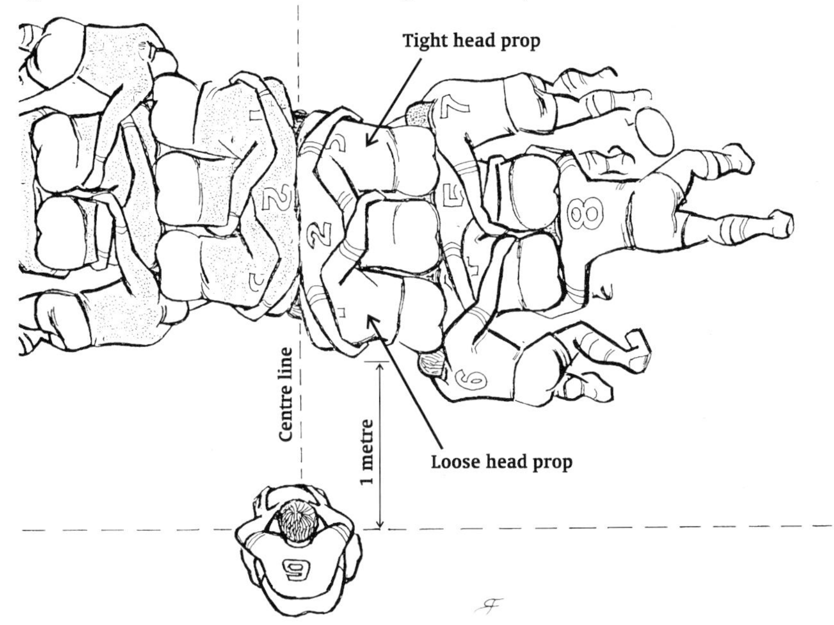

PLAN VIEW OF A SCRUMMAGE SHOWING THE CORRECT FORMATION.

1) Three in the front row, eight in each pack.
2) Loosehead packing to the left of opposing tighthead.
3) Front row heads in alternate positions.

BINDING IN THE SCRUMMAGE.

In 1996 a law change made it illegal for players to break away from the scrummage before the ball was out. This was introduced with a view to creating more space around the perimeter of the scrummage, giving the attacking side more options. It had been common practice for teams to "drop off" one, or even two of the back row forwards, when defending against their opponent's put in. Having confidence in the ability of their front five forwards to hold the shove, the loose forwards would stand on-side, just behind the back foot of the second row and form a defensive wall. Backed up by the scrum-half, they successfully managed to "snuff-out" most opposition moves tried close to the scrummage. The new law prevents this happening, stating that back row players must remain properly bound on for the duration of the scrummage. As a result, instead of running into a wall of defenders, the ball carrier is now more likely to confront a one-to-one situation. This is in line with RFU objectives and will only work if the referees ensure that all eight forwards in the scrummage bind on correctly and continuously until the scrummage is over.

To bind correctly a player must have the whole of one arm, from hand to shoulder, firmly around the body of a team mate. The only player who can legally bind onto a player of the opposing side is a prop-forward. Priority is always given to the hooker in the scrummage, because he has the responsibility of winning the ball. He may bind with his arms over, or under the arms of his props. Most hookers choose to bind over their prop's arms, as this places them in a more forward position and therefore nearer to the ball. What he cannot do, is to bind with one over and the other under. This used to be common practice in the past, allowing the hooker to twist his body and get nearer to his opponents ball, but it has now been stopped because it was the reason for many collapsed scrummages. Whether he chooses to bind over or under, his hands must still firmly grasp both props under the armpits, so that he cannot swing in the tunnel.

When the scrummage engages, the tighthead prop must bind on the opposing loosehead prop by placing his right arm outside the left upper arm of the loosehead and reaching for his body. He is allowed to grip the opposing prop's shirt, but his hand must be more towards the back of his opponent, rather than underneath in the chest area. He should not exert any downward pressure with this arm. The loosehead prop may either bind on the tighthead prop by placing his arm inside his opponent's right arm, or place his left hand, or forearm on his own left thigh. Under no circumstances should the referee allow either prop to place an outside hand into the tunnel, any such action would only be for the purpose of foul play. It is equally important to ensure that no player is allowed to grasp a prop by the leg, as such an action is likely to cause the scrummage to collapse.

The secondrow forwards bind together with their inside arms and use their outside arms to bind onto the frontrow. This they usually do by placing their arms between the legs of their respective prop-forwards and grabbing the shorts waist-band, or the shirt. Relationships need to be more than a little harmonious for this, the most intimate of binds.

The remaining three backrow forwards have a variety of positions where they may legally join onto the front five forwards, but whichever they choose they must bind on using the whole of at least one arm. They are not allowed to bind onto the frontrow, as only three players are allowed there at any time, but they can bind onto the second row, or create a third row.

This still gives the more creative teams quite a few options. The traditional scrummage formation is 3 frontrow; 4 secondrow; 1 thirdrow, but alternative variations have included the following 3-2-3; 3-3-2, and even a 3-5-0 formation. Such unusual formations have come about during the last season in an attempt to negate the fact that all forwards had to remain bound onto the scrummage until the ball was out. By playing five players in the second row one of them was therefore placed in a very loose position, not a lot different from where he would have chosen to stand, when the law allowed him to drop off the scrummage.

The law for the 1997/98 season has addressed this matter and has stated that the player whose feet are the "hindmost" feet in the scrummage must bind with at least one arm onto one of his locks. This will prevent the possibility of a legal 3-5-0 formation in the future. However the players form up in the scrummage, the most important thing is for the referee to ensure that all eight of each side remain down, properly and continuously bound on, while the ball is in the scrummage, so that space for attacking players is available.

After one complete season the signs are encouraging, because first division tries scored in 1996/97 totalled 745, which is 343 (or 85%) more than scored in the previous season, before the law changed.

THE BALL IN THE SCRUMMAGE

When the two packs have engaged the hooker must have both feet on the ground, with his weight firmly on one foot and his foremost foot must not be in front of the feet of his props. He should remain in this position and not raise his striking foot until the ball leaves the hands of the player putting it into the scrummage. When putting the ball in, the scrumhalf should stand one metre from the scrummage and midway between the two front rows, where the prop's shoulders meet. The ball should be held with both hands at a level midway between the knee and ankle. From this position the ball should be put in without any delay, or without feint, or backward movement. The put in should be a single forward movement, at a quick speed, straight along the middle line, so that it first touches the ground immediately beyond the width of the nearer prop's shoulders. His opposite number is allowed to stand beside him while the ball is being put in. If the ball, having been put in, comes out at either end of the tunnel, it should be put in again, but if it comes out anywhere behind a prop's foot play should continue.

Once the ball is in the scrummage, the scrumhalf who's team did not win possession, must keep both of his feet behind the ball, in order to remain on-side. Providing he complies with this, he is allowed to advance down the side of the scrummage as the ball is moved back towards the number eight. He is not allowed to advance in the same way on the other side of the scrummage, nor is he allowed to drift sideways away from it. He must remain in close proximity to the scrummage, which in the eyes of most referees will mean within three or four feet.

There had been a tendency for the scrumhalves to move sideways away from the scrummage to take up a position directly in front of the opposing flyhalf. While having the privilege of using the ball as the off-side line, they were able to get very close, especially when the flyhalves chose to take up the more favoured flat formation. If the scrumhalves wish to mark the opposing flyhalf now, they must retire behind the back foot of the hindmost player in their pack. This law was introduced in 1996 at the same time as it was decided that all forwards had to remain bound on to the scrummage. These two changes have successfully created more space for attacking players in the previously congested area around the perimeter of the scrummage. The additional freedom of movement afforded to scrumhalves poses a big threat to the side who have won possession, as they are allowed to advance down the side of the scrum, just inches behind the ball. Being this close can make life very difficult for the player trying to pick the ball up. However, as they are only allowed to advance in this way on the side that the ball was put in, the forwards usually channel the ball diagonally across the scrum, so that it comes to rest just to the right hand side of the number eight. In this way, they give the ball the maximum protection from the opposing predatory scrum-half. As this player must remain behind the ball it is impossible for him to get around the body and legs of the number eight and stay on-side.

While the ball lies in this position, between the right leg of the number eight and the left leg of the wing forward, the referee will rule that it is still in the scrum. But at the same time he will not penalise a player of the side in possession if they choose to play the ball. – A clear case of having one's cake and eating it as well! If a member of the opposing team attempts to play the ball while it is in the same position, he would be penalised for handling the ball in the scrum. Such positive discrimination towards the side in possession, greatly improves their chances of getting the ball away cleanly.

The team in possession still have to be careful, because the very second that a member of their team places a hand on the ball the scrummage will be judged to have ended. At this time all off-side lines disappear and the opposition can advance. Should the scrum-half place his hand on the ball and then change his mind, withdrawing without the ball, he should be penalised for handling in the scrummage.

While the ball is in the scrummage, all of the players who are not directly involved have to remain behind the off-side line, which is an imaginary line drawn just behind the feet of the hindmost forward in each pack and parallel to the goal lines.

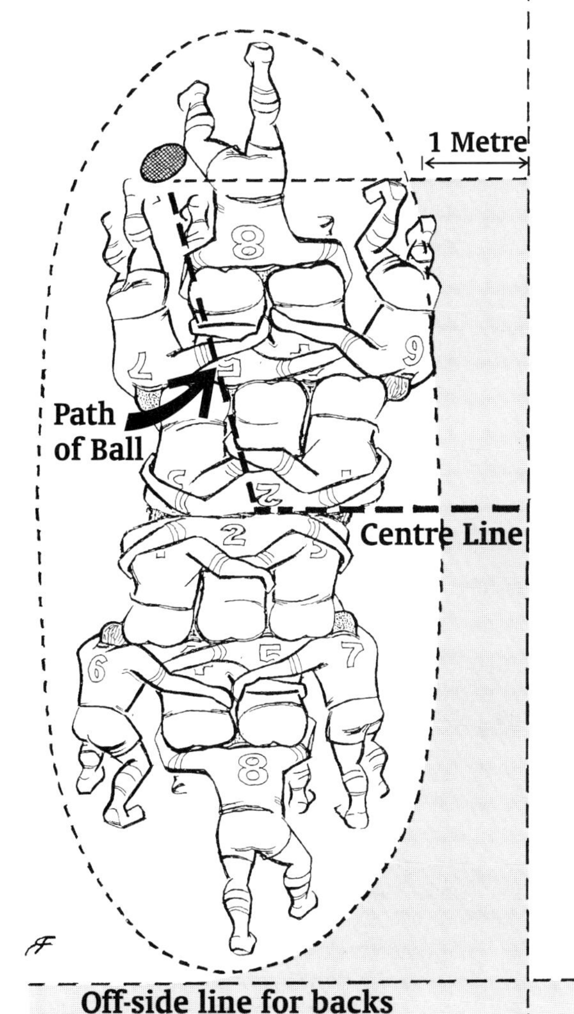

PLAN VIEW OF A SCRUMMAGE, SHOWING THE PATH OF THE BALL

The shaded area is the area which can be legally occupied by the scrum-half who did not put in the ball. He cannot go beyond the line of the ball (a line which advances as the ball progresses through the scrummage), and must not stray wider than 1 metre from the scrummage, unless he is behind his own No. 8.

WHO COLLAPSED THE SCRUMMAGE?

The scrummage is a potential problem area for all referees, aggravated by the fact, that the majority of them, have never played in the front row. Even referees who have played in a forward position, still find the scrummage difficult to manage, for the following reasons:

- They are a means of gaining possession, which is a priority for players.
- Players are forced into direct physical contact with their opponent.
- They are recurring throughout the game.
- Many players are involved.
- If they collapse, they are dangerous and can be life threatening.

The last of these reasons is the cause of most concern because, the players' safety is paramount. For this reason, whenever a scrummage collapses, the referees are advised to blow their whistles immediately, in order to minimize the possibility of injuries. Having stopped the game, they should then take action to reduce the chance of it happening again. Working out who caused the scrummage to collapse, or why it collapsed, is not an easy task. In the first instance, one should not forget that it can often be purely circumstantial:

- Conditions under foot may be slippery
- A player might loose his balance
- The players might be tired and exhausted
- One pack might be much heavier than their opponents.

Alternatively, it could be the result of poor coaching and/or bad technique: Loose binding

- Incorrect body positioning
- Inadequate footwear
- One player being more experienced or "streetwise" than his opponent.

Finally, it should also be remembered, that it is possible for any of the four props and probably the two hookers as well, to deliberately bring a scrummage down single handed, if and when they choose.

No matter what the reason might be for the collapse of a scrummage, it is very important that the referee assesses the situation correctly and quickly, because all collapsed scrummages are dangerous. This is particularly so if they are being collapsed repeatedly and deliberately.

The most common cause of a collapsed scrummage is loose binding and although this can often be attributed to poor technique, or fatigue, it can also be deliberate. The most common example being the hooker who slips his bind, in order to lower his body into the tunnel and get nearer to the ball. This can be spotted by looking on top of the scrummage, where the referee will notice a gaping hole where the hooker's body should be. The solution is to ensure that all players are binding with the whole arm, hands are under their team-mate's armpits and that they remain like that throughout the scrummage. A second problem area, that can also be resolved before the ball is put in, is the angle of the player's backs. The law makes it clear, that no player in the scrummage can pack with his shoulders below the level of his hips. This is easily spotted from the side of the scrummage and should be corrected before the ball is put in.

So if the binding is correct – The players all have flat backs – All circumstantial reasons are eliminated and the scrummage still collapses, what can be done? The referee must now determine which of the players is deliberately taking the scrummage down. He should be looking out for the little "tell tale signs" such as: Who had most to gain by the collapse? Who was first to release his bind? Who is in the most comfortable position on the ground? All of these are valuable clues that might enable the referee to confidently pick out the culprit.

If the referee knows who caused the scrummage to collapse, he should penalize him and consider a caution, or sending off.

If the referee *thinks* he knows who caused the scrummage to collapse, he should penalize his suspect.

If the referee has no idea (and this can happen to the very best referees) then although he is in a very difficult position, the worst thing that he could do, is nothing. Some referees choose to guess – some alternate penalties – some award the penalty to the side who are unable to score directly from the kick – others pick on tight head props, as they are generally thought to be the aggressors.

None of these solutions are very satisfactory and the more prudent referees resort to the use of preventative tactics. One such method, which has been known to work, is to exaggerate the shoulders above the hips ruling. By insisting on this, before allowing the ball to be put in, the referee can create a scrummage, where it is physically impossible for the front rows to go down. Instead, they find themselves going up towards a standing position, every time pressure is exerted. As they dislike such unnatural positioning very much, they quickly settle down and become "good boys", enabling the referee to allow the game to resort to norm.

Having read this article, it is hoped that you will appreciate that the answer to the question, "Who collapsed the scrummage?" is not easy to answer. It is also hoped, that you will in future be sympathetic towards the referee, while he strives to find the correct solution, in the interest of the players' safety and the continuity of the game.

SAFETY IN THE SCRUMMAGE

In today's world many professional people in positions of authority, such as teachers, police, doctors etc., run the risk of being sued for damages, for actions taken in good faith while carrying out their jobs. Referee Societies have been concerned for some time that this could happen to one of their members and in October 1991 it did!

On this day a young 17 year old hooker broke his neck playing for Sutton Coldfield Colts against Burton-upon-Trent Colts and as a result he was unfortunately paralysed from the neck down. The injury occurred when a scrummage collapsed and the injured party claimed, through the courts, that the referee failed to control the match and exposed the players to unnecessary risk by allowing scrummages to collapse repeatedly. In court a judgement was made against the referee and considerable damages were awarded. The case is presently under consideration for an appeal.

This was the first case of its kind to reach the courts in Britain and it could have a devastating effect on the game of Rugby Football. All volunteer referees for school and junior club rugby will now think twice before picking up a whistle, knowing that there is a risk of such action. The RFU recognise the importance of safe practices on the field for all players and particularly the juniors, who are not fully developed. That is why the 'Rugby Continuum' was produced in 1990. (Ironically one year before this tragic accident).

The Continuum is a book of rules that amend the laws of the game to suit the development of young players. Those of 7 years and under do not scrummage. Their games are re-started with a free pass by the non-offending side. At the age of 8 years the children are introduced to the concept of scrummaging by the forming of uncontested scrums. Such scrums are made up of one row containing three players from each team, and the side who are awarded the put-in must win the ball. This might seem pointless, but as the scrums are static, it allows the referee/coach to ensure that each front row is binding firmly together, all shoulders are above hips, and nothing happens that might cause a scrummage to collapse. When the children reach the age of 10 years the scrummages still only contain three players from each team, but they are now allowed to push and strike for the ball, with a view to gaining possession. At the age of 12 years, two second row players are added, making a total of five in each pack, all other rules being the same as before. Only at the age of 13 years do the teams contain 15 players, with eight a side in the scrummage. This gradual introduction to the techniques and pressures of scrummaging gives the children every chance of establishing their suitability for a position in the front row, with the minimal risk of injury.

By way of an additional safety measure all children under the age of 19 have to go through a set routine prior to the engagement of every scrum, and those who are entitled to push may only advance 1.5 metres. Once the packs are formed correctly, the referee should insist that the front row players CROUCH, then TOUCH their immediate opponent on the shoulder, or upper arm, PAUSE in this position until invited to ENGAGE. This repeated routine of CROUCH-TOUCH-PAUSE and ENGAGE, ensures that the players adopt the correct positions, and it also prevents

the possibility of one pack charging at the other.

Let us hope that all the Youth Development Officers, Pilkington Training Officers; Junior Club Coaches, and school masters are aware of, and are enforcing, these safety measures so that we do not read of another tragic accident.

In the senior game (over 19 year olds) safety in the scrummage is still a major concern, endorsed by the recent change to the laws regarding the replacement of front row forwards. If for whatever reason, a team are unable to field a specialist front row player when one was required, then the game should continue with non-contested scrummages. These are the same as conventional scrummages except that: There is no contest for the ball. The team putting in the ball must win it. Neither team is permitted to push. The formation of both teams must be 3-4-1.

All of these measures have been introduced with safety in mind. One must remember that non-contestable scrummaging is only ever introduced when at least one member of the front row is not a regular front row. In this way such a player is never put under any pressure that might cause him injury.

For league and cup games in England there are certain competition rules to deter teams from claiming non-contestable scrummaging as a method of negating their opponents superiority in this department. If the referee has to order non-contestable scrummaging, because a team was unable to replace the first front row that had to retire, that team would sacrifice the match no matter what the score. On occasions when a team, having replaced one front row forward, are unable to provide a second, the referee should again order non-contestable scrummaging, but the final score would stand.

Other scrummaging safety issues in the senior game are related to the engagement, binding and collapsing, all of which are covered in the four preceding articles.

FORMING A LINEOUT

The lineout is used to restart a game of rugby after the ball has gone into touch. On most occasions the team not responsible for causing the ball to go into touch, have the right to throw the ball in. This is an advantage because they are able to choose how many players make-up the lineout, where to throw and the velocity of the throw. Combined with many hours of training it is now unusual for a first division team to loose possession of the ball on it's own throw.

When a team are awarded a penalty kick and they elect to kick directly into touch, the throw-in at the resulting lineout should be awarded to them. This exception is designed to enhance the power of the penalty as a deterrent to foul play.

On the rare occasions when the touch judge, nor the referee, can decide who was responsible for making the ball go into touch, the throw should be awarded to the attacking side; which by RFU definition, means the team who are not in their own half of the field.

The place for a throw-in is called the "line of touch", which is an imaginary line running across the field of play, parallel to the goal lines, at the place indicated by the touch judge. Each team must line up half a metre on it's own side of this line, so as to leave a clear space of one metre between the two lines of players.

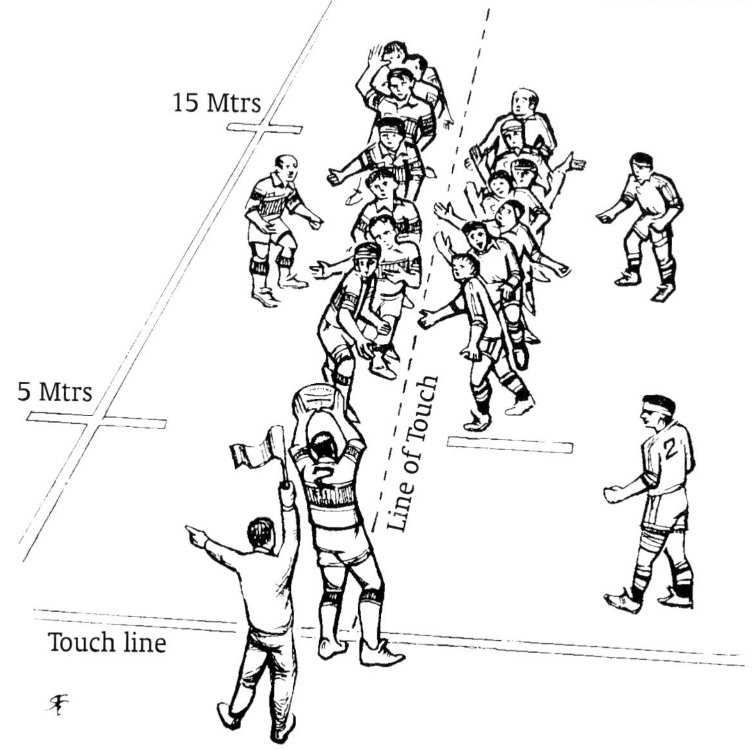

At least two players from each team are required to form a lineout and the maximum number is determined by the team who have the right to throw the ball in. The conventional number of players in a lineout is seven, but if the team throwing in the ball choose to reduce the number, then the opposition must also. Failure to do so would entitle the side throwing in the ball to have a free-kick awarded on the line of touch, fifteen metres in from touch. All players in the lineout must stand between the five metre line and the fifteen metre line. Any player who is further than fifteen metres from the touch line when the lineout begins is not in the lineout.

The ball is usually thrown in by the hooker, who's immediate opponent should remain within five metres of the touchline on his own side of the line of touch. Once the ball has been thrown in five metres, the two hookers can join the lineout. One other player from each team (usually the scrum-half) is allowed to take up a position to receive the ball if it is passed, or knocked back from the lineout.

All other players are not participating in the lineout and must remain at least ten metres back from the line of touch. When the ball is in touch players who approach the line-of-touch must always be presumed to do so for the purpose of forming a lineout. This is a requirement so that the team who are not throwing-in the ball, have every chance to establish how many players they can place in the lineout.

The lineout starts the instant the ball leaves the hands of the player who is throwing it.

SUPPORTING OR LIFTING?

The law has always made it clear that a player cannot be lifted off the ground by a team mate in the lineout, but it has been less precise about what the supporting players can do. Two significant changes were made to the laws before the start of the 1996/97 season, which made it legal for the supporting player to assist the jumper. Previously the law had stated that it was illegal for a player in the lineout to bind on any other player of his own team before the ball had been touched by a player participating in the lineout. As this clause was omitted in 1996 it was logical to assume that there would then be no such restriction on players standing in the line. Secondly, the law added that a player should not support any player of his own team before that player had jumped for the ball. Again, logic would indicate that it therefore, would be legal to do so once he had jumped.

At this time it appeared that we were going into the new season knowing that players were free to bind on members of their own team at any time during the lineout and that they could also support a jumping player providing he had left the ground under his own steam. Things that had been going on unpunished and/or unnoticed for many years were now made legal and crystal clear. It was hoped that the introduction of these changes would provide a clean and fair contest for the ball in future lineouts.

Well law is one thing – interpretation is another! Unfortunately, it all went terribly wrong when the coaches from Divisions 1 and 2 met with referees from the National Referee Development Squad on the 29th of September 1996 to discuss the new laws. During the course of this meeting those, assembled agreed on the following incredible interpretation for the new lineout laws:

- There was to be no restriction on where the jumping player, who has left the ground unaided, could be supported.

It is difficult to understand, how the top coaches, together with the national referee development squad, could collectively agree on an interpretation of law that was so obviously open to abuse. However, it happened and all clubs and officials were informed in the same month.

Every time a new law is introduced the more inventive coaches and players apply their minds to find out ways in which they might bend the rules, in order to gain an advantage over their opponents – they had a field day with this one! At first the supporting players were holding the jumpers by the bottom of their shorts and found that they could gain a few inches in height. It was then discovered that, with practise, a smaller but more gymnastic jumper could compete with a bigger man, provided he was "supported" at his lower thigh, or knee area. Of course it was not long before some supporters were cupping their hands, jockey style, and giving their jumper a leg-up. The lineout was beginning to resemble a circus act.

This obviously could not be allowed to continue, not only because the law was being flaunted but because the jumpers were reaching such heights that there was a risk of very serious injury, should they loose their balance. For this reason, a further meeting was held on the 9th of October 1996, when it was agreed that it would not be legal for supporting players to hold the jumper anywhere below his waist. The previous interpretation had only lasted 10 days and it was left to the referees to sort out the confusion between the coaches and the players.

The referees were all briefed on how to interpret this law and on exactly what the supporting player could legal do. The agreement was that support may take place only when the ball has been thrown in and when the jumper is off the ground by his own means. Any such support should be above the jumper's waist and the supporting player should have open flat hands, with his fingers pointing upwards.

Seeing big men such as England's Martin Johnson and Simon Shaw leaping high in the air to secure possession in the lineouts is pretty spectacular and, not surprisingly, frequently attracts the attention of the sports photographer. Of all the photographs featured in the newspapers, magazines and programmes, that I have seen since the beginning of the 1996/97 season, there has not been one in which the players are supporting legally. (see Cover photograph) It would appear, that the referees are so relieved that supporting in the lineout has almost eliminated the more serious offences committed across the line of touch that they are turning their blind eye to the illegal supporting – or is it lifting?

LIFTING

SUPPORTING

The players are becoming so efficient at support play that the jumpers are now able to "hover" when at the peak of their jump. This ability has brought about another illegal practice that is going unnoticed or ignored by the referees. The players throwing in the ball are now waiting until their jumper is in "hover mode" and then throwing the ball directly to him. This is a clear cut case of cheating, because jumpers cannot "hover" without the aid of support and the law clearly states that support should not take place before the ball is thrown in. But who can blame the players or coaches if referees are electing not to referee it.

Another law change in 1996 gave the jumpers a little more freedom. Previously jumpers had been restricted to using both hands, or their inside hand, to play the ball in the lineout. This was introduced to stop jumpers illegally obstructing their opponents with their inside arm while playing the ball with their outside arm. Although this did help towards stopping illegal contact across the line it also prevented players from using their favoured hand, be it left, or right. The law has been changed to allow the jumpers the freedom of playing the ball with either hand, providing both of their arms are above their heads.

THE QUICK THROW IN

Players have been allowed to take a throw-in quickly, without waiting for a lineout to form, for many years, but such a throw had to be taken from the line of touch exactly where the ball had crossed the touch-line. In an attempt to make the game more exciting and reduce the amount of stoppage time, the RFU introduced a new law in 1992 allowing players to take a quick throw-in from anywhere on the touch-line, between the place where the ball went into touch and their own goal-line. This offered the side with the right to throw-in additional attacking options, but they could only take advantage provided they complied with other conditions.

A quick throw-in is not allowed if the lineout has already been formed. (One is deemed to have been formed when two or more players from each side are lined up on either side of the line of touch, in readiness for the throw-in to take place.) The ball that went into touch is the only ball that can be used, and that ball must not have been touched by anyone else except the player taking the throw. If a replacement ball is used, or the quick throw-in taken after a lineout is formed, then the quick throw-in is disallowed and the same team would throw-in back at the lineout, as indicated by the touch judge.

When taking a quick throw-in, the ball, as for a normal lineout, must be thrown in straight so that it travels at least five metres before it touches the ground or another player. Failure to comply with these conditions would mean that the quick throw-in would be disallowed and the opposing team given the choice of a throw-in at the place where the quick throw-in was attempted, or a scrum 15 metres in on the same line.

The place where a player might attempt a quick throw-in and the place where a lineout should be formed could be 50 metres or more apart, making life very difficult for the referee. For this reason the RFU have asked touch judges to assist by not raising their non-flag carrying arm, to indicate who should throw-in, until after the right to take a quick throw-in has gone. In this way the referee can tell, with a quick glance at his touch judge, whether a quickly taken throw-in was legal or otherwise. The ball boys are also instructed not to field a ball that a player might wish to retrieve and throw in quickly.

By the way, it is possible for a player to throw the ball in quickly to himself, providing the throw-in is straight, and travels at least five metres before it touches the ground.

Quick throw-ins have been allowed for four years, provided the same ball is used, and only the player throwing in has touched it. It was therefore thought by most referees that a quick throw-in should never be allowed when a ball carrier has been forced into touch since the tackled player and the thrower must both have handled the ball in touch. Nothing changes these facts, but a directive from the RFU in 1996 stated that referees are to allow a quick throw-in to take place, even if a ball carrier has been forced into touch.

I believe the quick throw-in law, as introduced in 1992, is popular with players, coaches, referees and spectators, because it makes a big contribution towards keeping the game alive and more exciting. Congratulations to the Law Makers again!

THE PLAYING ENCLOSURE

The referee has sole responsibility for the PLAYING ENCLOSURE during the course of a game, which includes the whole of the playing area, plus a reasonable space surrounding it. At a gate taking club this is the area inside the barriers. Clubs who are less fortunate are obliged to define this area by erecting ropes for all league and cup games. Each club is responsible for ensuring that all spectators, replacements and officials (with the exception of the touch judges) are kept at a reasonable distance from the field of play. People should only enter or leave this enclosure with the permission of the referee.

The FIELD OF PLAY is the area bound in by, but not including the goal lines and the touch lines.

The PLAYING AREA is the field of play, plus the two in-goal areas.

The touch lines are in touch, so if the ball carrier places a foot on the line, the ball is out of play.

The goal lines are in-goal, so if an attacking player grounds the ball on this line, a try should be awarded.

The dead-ball line is not in in-goal, so if a ball carrier places his foot on this line, he will have taken the ball out of play.

The touch-in-goal lines and the corner posts are in touch-in-goal, so if either is touched by an attacking ball carrier, before he is able to ground the ball for a try, he will be judged to have taken the ball out of play.

The goal posts are erected in the goal lines, so if an attacking player grounds the ball, so that the ball is touching both the post and the ground, a try should be awarded.

The twenty two metre lines are in the twenty two metre areas, which means that if the fullback's foot was on, but not over one of these lines when making a mark, the mark would be awarded.

Grass is the preferred playing surface, but the law makes concessions, stating that clay or sand may be used when grass is not available. The painting of advertisements on the playing surface is strictly prohibited.

The home club is responsible for marking out the pitch correctly and clearly. A very important job for which they are given a surprising amount of freedom. After stating that all areas are to be rectangular, the law then only provides the maximum dimensions for the length and width of the FIELD OF PLAY. The length must not exceed 100 metres and the width must not exceed 70 metres, giving the groundsman a lot of scope. This is rarely a problem in the higher leagues, as the pitches are all close to the maximum, but players at lower levels can be confronted with pitches that are long and narrow, or short and wide. It has not been unknown for clubs who are traditionally strong in the forwards to deliberately mark out a narrow pitch and clubs who are strong in the threequarters to have a wide pitch.

For the in-goal area the Law changes tack and gives the minimum distance that is required between the goal line and the dead ball line. It states that this distance should be not less than 10 metres – an interesting point indeed for those first division clubs who have seen fit to move into Soccer stadiums and are providing half the legal requirement of in-goal area.

Visiting teams do have the right to object about the ground or the markings, but any such objection must be made before the first kick-off.

IS THE BALL IN TOUCH?

This being rugby football, one would not expect the answer to the question, "Is the ball in touch?" to be straight forward and you would be correct. The important points to know are:

- The touch-lines and the corner flag posts are in touch.
- The ball is in touch under the following circumstances:
- When it is carried by a player and it, or the player, touches a touch-line or the ground beyond it.
- When it is not carried by a player and it touches the touch-line, or the ground beyond it.

Usually when the touch judge raises his flag a ball carrier has been bundled into touch by an opponent's tackle, or the ball has been kicked into the back row of the stand. Either way, there is little doubt that the ball should rightly be judged to be in touch. As the touch line itself is in touch, the ball should be judged to be out of play if it bounces on it, or if the ball-carrier places a foot on it.

Now you know the general rules of the game, here are four situations to make you think. Remembering the guidelines previously given, if you were the touch judge, would you raise your flag?

1) A player starting with both feet well in the field-of-play jumps upwards and outwards beyond the plane of the touch-line and knocks the ball (that was in the air several feet beyond the plane of the touch-line) back towards his own goal line and into play, before coming back to ground.

2) The ball is kicked into the air and travels several yards beyond the plane of the touch-line. While still in the air it is 'picked-up' by a very strong cross wind and blown back into the field of play, where it first bounces.

3) A player who is lying on the ground, with both of his legs in touch, reaches out with his hand and taps the ball back towards a player of his own team. The ball was positioned two feet in from the touch-line at the time it was tapped.

4) A player standing with one foot in touch kicks the ball (which is lying well within the field of play) with his other foot.

Those of you that would not have raised the flag, on all of the above occasions, may congratulate yourselves, as you are correct. On no occasion was the ball in touch, for the following reasons:

1) The player jumped from within the field of play and did not make contact with the ground beyond the touchline until after he had played the ball. Also, the ball never made contact with the touch line or the ground beyond it.

2) The ball never touched the touch-line, or the ground beyond it and play should therefore continue.

3 & 4) Although on both occasions the player was in touch, he did not attempt to carry the ball and the ball never touched the touch-line or the ground beyond it.

So, if it is possible for a player to legally play the ball when he has part of his body in touch, providing he does not carry it, and as one only needs to apply downward pressure on the ball to score a try, the following conundrum is posed: Can a player who has his feet in touch score a legitimate try? What are your thoughts?

See page 75 for the correct answer.

PLAYERS' DRESS

The laws on players' dress have always been a little vague, leaving both players and referees unsure of exactly what is allowed. This has been magnified by advances made in modern technology and materials, resulting in numerous newly designed sports aids becoming available on the rapidly growing rugby consumer market.

The RFU have always treated the safety of the players as a priority and as they have become increasingly concerned about the potential dangers of some of the kit that is creeping into our game, the law on players' dress was completely rewritten in 1996. Previously the law simply stated one or two items that should not be worn. Now, the new law is presented in two sections, one clearly stating what a player may wear and the other equally clearly stating what he cannot wear, as follows:

SECTION 1 – PLAYERS MAY WEAR:

- A mouth guard.
- Shin guards provided they have no sharp edges.
- Pads of a soft material provided they are attached to the body by tape and not sewn into the garment.
- A scrum cap, or strips of tape as a protection for the ears. Only the RHINO and GILBERT scrum caps are approved.
- Mitts
- Bandages, or a dressing to cover an open or bleeding wound sustained during a match.

SECTION 2 – PLAYERS MAY NOT WEAR:

- Shoulder pads of the harness type.
- Braces, or supports which include any rigid, or reinforced material.
- Protective garments on any part of the body, except as in section 1.
- Helmets, or head guards, except as in section 1.
- Undergarments which include padding
- Clothing which has become bloodstained during the match
- Gloves
- Dangerous projections, such as buckles, or rings

Players' studs are also covered by this law and they should be British Standard BS6366, or else moulded rubber.

The RFU were hoping that the newly written law would provide clarity and eliminate confusion. They also clearly state that players who require any form of protection or support as listed in section 2 above, should not be playing the game of Rugby Football for their own safety.

The referee retains the power to decide before or during the match that any part of a player's dress is dangerous and he can insist on its removal before the player resumes play. Also if the referee or touch judge has already indicated to a player on inspection before the match that an item was inadmissible under the new law, and the player is then found to be wearing it on the field-of-play, then that player should be ordered off under law 26. This law covers misconduct that is prejudicial to the spirit of good sportsmanship and is a red card offence. Such offences would therefore be referred to the disciplinary panel, who would probably restrict that player from playing for a further three or four weeks.

Unfortunately, despite the best intentions of the RFU, the new clearly worded law covering players' dress has been completely ignored by the majority of the senior referees. This lack of discipline among the senior ranks will cause problems that will run on into next season. It will now be very difficult to persuade a player that he cannot wear the body harness that he has been allowed to wear throughout the previous season, if the law has not changed.

The law did not change throughout the 1996/97 season and it remains the same for the beginning of the next season, so let us hope that the senior referees do not continue to shirk their responsibilities and they get into the changing rooms and stop this growing problem, before the players start shopping in American Football shops.

In fairness to our referees, it should be pointed out that this is an International problem, in which the Southern Hemisphere Countries are leading the way; making it all the more difficult to believe that we are all playing to the same set of International Laws. It will not have gone unnoticed by youngsters in this country just how many players, both British and South African, chose to wear body harnesses during the 1997 Lions Tour. What law was being applied by these referees?

REPLACEMENT AND SUBSTITUTION OF PLAYERS

The replacement of players was first introduced in the 1970's, when only two were allowed and they could only be used to replace an injured player. On such occasions the injury would have to be confirmed by a medically trained person, or in the absence of a doctor, by the referee. This precaution was always open to abuse, as not many doctors were prepared to rule that a player was fit to play, if the player himself did not agree. As for the referees, I am able to tell you, as the Referee Training Officer for Leicestershire, that all local referees are advised never to challenge a player who declares himself unfit.

As the game developed and we had the introduction of leagues, knock-out cups and then professionalism, the clubs demanded more replacements. The lawmakers obliged and at the start of the 1996/97 season a first division team could nominate four replacements, all of whom could be played providing the player coming off was injured, or had a bleeding wound.

On the 4th November 1996 the replacement law was changed again, making it possible for the team coach to make tactical substitutions. From that time English teams were able to nominate up to 19 players for a game, 15 to start and up to four on the bench. Before the end of the 1996/97 the laws for English league rugby were changed yet again to bring them in line with the law for international games. We go into the 1997/98 season with the replacement law as follows:

Teams will be allowed to nominate up to 21 players prior to the game. Of these 21 players, 5 must be capable of playing in the front row. On occasions when only 19, or 20 players are nominated, the teams are still obliged to have 5 capable of playing in the front row. When 16, 17, or 18 players are nominated then 4 must be capable of playing in the front row.

This has been introduced for safety reasons and in order to reduce the chances of a game ending with non-contested scrummaging. A team who nominated 19 players and then claimed they would not be able to replace a front-row forward who was injured, or ordered off, would be deemed to have lost the match regardless of the score. If a team had replaced two injured frontrow forwards and were unable to replace a third, the referee would allow non-contested scrummaging and the final score would stand.

In the event of a front row forward being ordered off, the referee, in the interest of safety, should confer with the captain of his team to determine whether another player was suitably trained and experienced to take his position; if not the captain should nominate another forward to leave the playing area and the referee will permit a substitute front row forward to replace him. This may take place immediately, or after another player has been tried in that position. When there is no front row forward available for whatever reason the game should continue with non-contestable scrummaging. This is the same as contested scrummaging except that:

- There is no contest for the ball.
- The team putting in the ball must win it.
- Neither team is allowed to push.
- The formation of both teams must be 3-4-1.

Besides being used for the replacement of injured players, the 6 men on the bench can now be used as tactical substitutes. Up to 2 substitutes of front-row players and up to 4 substitutes of other players may be made, for any reason, but only when the ball is dead and with the permission of the referee.

A player that is substituted may not himself be later used as a substitute, but can go on to cover for a player who has an open or bleeding wound. Players that have been replaced because of injury can not legally resume playing under any circumstances in the same game. Any objection by either team regarding the number of players in a team may be made to the referee at any time, but such objections will not affect the score previously obtained.

Substitution in our game is revolutionary and it will be very interesting to see how it develops. Will the coaches use it to replace a struggling prop, a shaky full-back under the high ball, a kicker having an off day, or will he simply put on four pairs of fresh legs in the last twenty minutes? We shall see!

BLOODY RULES

As recently as 1994, when a player took a knock, or was cut, the decision as to whether he should continue to play or not was based solely on the risks to that individual. On many occasions we have seen players allowed to continue with blood flowing from wounds that were considered not to be life threatening or in a dangerous position.

For many players it was a point of honour that they should not leave the field and abandon their team-mates. I have witnessed many a burly forward pleading with the referee to allow him to remain on the field of play, especially before the 1980's when no replacements were allowed.

That is not to say that the modern player is any less honourable, because unfortunately, we have all now had to adapt our lives in order to take precautions against such deadly viruses as AIDS and Hepatitis 'B', both of which are blood borne.

The first priority of the referee has always been the safety of the players and as these viruses are transferable from blood to blood, anyone who is bleeding in a contact sport becomes a threat to all of the other players.

The RFU were very quick to recognise the risks and introduced a law allowing a bleeding player to be temporarily replaced until the bleeding was controlled and the wound covered or dressed. In the first instance such a player could only be replaced for ten minutes, and if he did not resume playing within that time the replacement become permanent. The ten minute period used to commence from the time the player left the playing area.

A further amendment ruled that a player with a bleeding wound could only be temporarily replaced once. These two rulings were extremely difficult for the referee and his touch judges to manage on top of all their other responsibilities and the Medical Committee were very concerned about the safety of the players. In 1995 on the advice of the Medical Committee, it was decided to remove the restriction on the number of occasions and the length of time that a temporary replacement may be used whilst bleeding wounds were being treated. A wise move, taking away the risk of players resuming play before their treatment was complete and removing unnecessary pressure on medical staff.

Players who have been replaced because of injury cannot under any circumstances take any further part in the same game and players who have been substituted cannot themselves go back on as straight substitutes, but they can be used as temporary replacements for bleeding players.

Leicester is a club that has taken the threat of Hepatitis 'B' very seriously and all of the players have been immunised against it. Another noticeable change brought about by the threat of blood borne viruses is the trend for rugby clubs to replace the much lampooned communal bath with showers – whatever next?

Looking around the First and Second Division Clubs they all seam to be quite well equipped to deal with the extra medical demands brought about because of the threat of aids, but this is not the case in junior rugby circles. One of the very first safety precautions was to outlaw the bucket and sponge. In the past, the old magic sponge had been the cure for everything, whether it be a black eye or a groin strain, a bruised rib or a cut to the head.

I am still very involved with local rugby, especially the juniors who play on Sunday mornings, and I am alarmed by the number of times I find that the only medical aid provided is a bucket and sponge. The clubs have all been made aware of the dangers to their players of using the bucket and sponge and yet they still persist. If there is a benefactor out there who would like to spend some of his money helping the game of Rugby Football to develop and at the same time possibly prevent a tragic accident, then the provision of complete purpose made first aid kits for junior clubs would be money very well spent. Something urgently needs to be done in this area, because the problem is prevalent throughout the country.

MAY I LEAVE THE FIELD SIR?

Before each game the referee should ask the teams if they had any medically trained people available. If so, suitably trained staff could be given permission to come onto the field to treat injured players while the game was in progress. Without such special permission, granted before the game, other people such as coaches, baggage attendants, doctors and first aid personnel must only come on when summoned by the referee.

Once the game has started the players are not allowed to leave the playing enclosure without the permission of the referee and this used to apply even to the period of time allotted for half-time. However, the law has changed this season and there can now be an interval of up to ten minutes, during which the players may leave the playing enclosure. According to the RFU, this change has been made to suit the demands of the modern game. Others think it has more to do with the demands of Sky TV.

Any player that is permitted to leave the playing enclosure for treatment to an injury or some other special circumstance

(I am tempted to tell you the story of a past-president of the Tigers who had to leave the field for a call of nature) must not resume playing until the referee has given him permission, and this will only be done while the ball is dead.

Any player who wilfully comes back on to the field without the referee's permission, in order to assist his team or obstruct an opponent, could be penalised for misconduct, which is an ordering off offence. If the offence was judged not to be wilful interference, but the offending team gained an advantage, the referee should order a scrummage to the non-offending team at the place where the player resumed playing without his permission.

In the modern game all sorts of people seem to want to get in on the act and run onto the playing enclosure. We have ball-boys, club mascots, people carrying kicking tees and the water-bottle man. The latter has become such a nuisance that the RFU have issued a new ruling stating that water carriers are not allowed to enter the playing area and must remain beyond the touchline, touch-in-goal-line and dead ball line. The players, on medical advice, are encouraged to drink water during a match and, although still not allowed to leave the playing area, may meet with the water carriers around the perimeter of the ground for this purpose.

ABANDONED GAMES

Abandoned rugby games are few and far between, but Leicester supporters will recall an incident in a recent Pilkington cup match at Exeter which came very close to being abandoned. It was a murky December day with a three o'clock kick off and the lights failed midway through the second half. The referee played on, but just as conditions were beginning to look impossible the power was restored and the game ran its natural course. However it did pose the question. What should be done if a League or Cup game is abandoned?

The answer is, as you would expect, clearly covered by the laws of the game. The referee has the power to declare no-side before time has expired if in his opinion the full time cannot be played, or if the continuance of play would be dangerous. If a league game is stopped because of weather conditions, or floodlight failure, the time of abandonment becomes crucial. If more than 60 minutes of rugby has been played (that is more than 20 minutes of the second half) then the score at the time of the abandonment becomes the match result. If less than 60 minutes has been played then the two teams should play again within 7 days.

The outcome of a game that is stopped for any reason other than weather conditions will be determined by the organising committee of the league concerned, irrespective of the number of minutes played, or the score at the time.

Referees are advised to think very carefully before ever abandoning a game because of foul play or the misconduct of the players. Such an action would in effect mean that ALL of the players had been ordered off, and all of them would therefore have to appear before a disciplinary committee. On occasions when the attitude of the players is such that the playing of the game is considered dangerous, the referee should stop the game, but he should make a point of naming the ringleaders only, who would probably have been cautioned previously.

ADVANTAGE

Until the year 1896 referees were simply used as adjudicators. The captains of the teams had, as in cricket, to appeal for a decision. Ironically it was this system which produced the advantage law which most distinguishes rugby football from other games. Obviously, no captain would appeal for a stoppage if his team had gained an advantage from an opponents mistake. In 1896 the practice of appeals was done away with and the referee became "the sole judge of fact and of law", as stated in the laws as they read today. Referees continued to apply the principle of advantage, established so long ago, by not whistling for an infringement which gains an advantage to the non-offending team.

The law states that an advantage must be either territorial or such possession of the ball as constitutes an obvious tactical advantage. A mere opportunity to gain advantage is not sufficient. This places a huge responsibility on the shoulders of the referee, for he alone judges whether an advantage has been gained or not. With the definite exception of foul play, the more artistic referees usually look for reasons NOT to blow their whistles.

However, I have to inform you, if you ever wanted to "stir up a hornet's nest" at a referees meeting, just ask for a few opinions on the advantage law! It is the one law where overall agreement is rarely achieved. Some of the most contentious aspects of the law being:

1) Is time relevant? How long do the non-offending team have to try and gain an advantage?
2) Should the referee signal that he is playing advantage, or does this give too big an advantage to the non-offending team?
3) Should the referee take into consideration the individual skills of the players on the field? e.g. A goal kicker who can score from the half way line.
4) Should the referee try to play advantage to the defending team following a penalty offence in their own 22 metre area?
5) Should the referee vary the amount of advantage he plays according to the temper of the game?

The referees can't agree on answers to the above, which explains why it is very much an art and not a science, and why there will always be inconsistencies from one referee, to another.

A referee is not allowed to play the advantage law under the following circumstances:

1) When the ball, or the player carrying it, touches the referee. If This happens and one team gains an advantage, the game should be stopped and restarted with a scrummage to the side who were in possession at the time it happened.
2) When the ball emerges from either end of the tunnel at a scrummage, not having been played by a front-row forward. The game should be stopped and a re-scrum ordered.
3) When the ball is knocked on by an attacking player, and rolls into the in-goal area where it is then touched down by a defending player. The usual 22 metre drop-out should not be awarded and the game should be restarted with a scrummage at the place the ball was knocked-on.
4) A kick-off must be kicked from the correct place and by the correct form of kick. If this is not done the referee will order it to be taken again correctly.

FOUL PLAY

Foul Play covers misconduct, dangerous play, obstruction, retaliation, unfair play, repeated infringements and unsporting behaviour. All of equal importance. The game of rugby football has a history of being well disciplined and played in the spirit of good sportsmanship. And long may it continue!

With the introduction of professionalism, the "spirit" of the game is being put to the test more than ever before and the outcome will be in the hands of the players, coaches and referees.

The law gives no guidance as to what is prejudicial to the spirit of good sportsmanship, it is left to the interpretation of the referees. They should be on the look out for such things as :

- Players throwing away the ball to prevent opponents taking penalty kicks quickly.
- Number Eights holding the ball at the base of a scrummage in order to "run down the clock".
- Players using verbal abuse in an attempt to goad opponents into some form of retaliation.
- Players moving or shouting while opponents are taking a penalty kick at goal.
- Players protesting about the referee's decision making or competence.

Non of these are prevalent at the moment and the referees will ensure that it stays that way.

Unfair play includes Repeated infringements, an offence that has unfortunately flourished since the introduction of professionalism. This is hardly surprising. As in other sports such offences are commonly known as "professional fouls". While the penalty goal is worth three points, compared to five, or possibly seven, for a try, it is clear to see why defending teams, when close to their own goal line, are tempted to deliberately give away penalties by killing the flow of the ball.

After much debate the referees are responding in the best way they know how – by awarding penalty tries. This is done when the referee decides that, but for a series of illegal actions close to the goal line, a try would have probably been scored. In such situations the referee should warn the offending side, after the third offence is committed, that a penalty try may be awarded. If a further offence then occurs the referee will award a penalty try.

Misconduct and dangerous play are usually clear-cut offences and include such actions as, the striking of an opponent, the wilful kicking, trampling or tripping of an opponent, late tackles, and "stiff arm" tackles. It also includes scrummaging offences such as, charging into the scrummage, lifting an opponent off the ground, or wilfully causing the scrummage to collapse.

Under obstruction, the law states that it is illegal for a player to push, hold, or block any opponent who is not carrying the ball. These offences can be very difficult to detect as they occur "off the ball" and can be quite subtle. The referee would be looking for assistance from the trailing touch judge to spot such offences. (See The Touch Judge, on page 76)

All offences covered by law 26 are considered to be very serious and the referees are instructed to always caution or order off offending players at the time of the offence, before any other action is taken. If a player, having received a caution, then offends a second time, the referee has no alternative to ordering him off.

THE REFEREE

According to the law there should be a referee appointed by the Union for every match, but if there is no appointed referee one can be mutually agreed upon by the two teams. The referee is responsible for keeping the time, the score, and he should apply the laws fairly, without any variation or omission. He should give no instructions or advice to either team before the kickoff, and during the match should only consult with the two touch judges.

The referee is the sole judge of fact and of law and his decisions are binding on the players. He cannot alter a decision, except when given before he observes that a touch judge has raised his flag. During the match, no-one other than the players, the referee and the touch judges, are allowed within the playing enclosure, unless it is with the permission of the referee. No player should leave the playing enclosure without the referee's permission, and if one does leave the field, he must not resume playing in the match until the referee has given his blessing. The players must respect the authority of the referee and must (except in the case of the kick-off at the start of each half) stop playing at once, when he has blown his whistle.

Managing a game between thirty players, according to a set of complex laws, has never been an easy task; made even more difficult by the introduction of professionalism and the increased need for success in league and cup competitions. Being fully aware of the responsibility placed on the referees, the Rugby Football Union have installed a structure of County Societies who are responsible for the recruitment, training, grading and appointing of referees within their area.

As the standard of rugby varies tremendously between a local club third team and a first division side such as Leicester, or Bath, the referees are graded nationally within four broad categories. This is done so that a competent referee can be appointed to games of all levels. The referee grade bands are 'C-List', 'B-List', 'A-List' and 'RFU Panel'.

'C' grade referees cover the vast majority of local junior rugby games. The better referees within this category would be given up to Courage League level 9, which in Leicestershire for example, would include Coalville, Lutterworth, South Leicester and Kibworth.

Referees capable of taking more senior games are promoted to level 'B' and would generally referee games between Courage league level 9 and 6. The very best of the 'B' referees are selected on to a 'B1' grade by regional groups and they referee at league levels 4, 5 and 6. It is at this stage that referees begin to travel about the country on exchange so that they might be observed by RFU advisers. Those 'B' referees who show the potential to make the pinnacle of RFU panel are selected on to the 'A' list, and are regularly appointed to referee at Courage league levels 3, 4, 5 and 6.

The RFU Panel might be considered as the 'cream of the crop' as they referee County Championship games and Courage league Divisions 1, 2, and 3. From within this category about ten referees are selected for special attention in order to assess their potential at international level. Generally it takes around 8-10 seasons for the most talented of the referees to work their way to the top.

The games are usually naturally graded by the level of the league, but non league games are also graded. For instance, an Under 21 International is considered to be the equivalent of a First Division game, a Woman's International a Second Division game, a Services International a Third Division game, and an Under 16 Schools International a Fourth Division game.

For 2nd Teams and others, the accepted formula is that you add three levels on to the league level of the respective First XV. and a further two levels for each successive XV. In this way a Division Four 2nd XV would be graded as a League level 7 game. Such a system helps the Society Appointments Secretaries to appoint a competent referee to each game, even if it was an exchange to the other side of the country.

All county Societies are short of referees – so if you think you can do better than the man in the middle, please contact the secretary of your local county society – they will be pleased to welcome you into the fold.

EVOLUTION OF THE REFEREE

The present law book states that "During a match the referee is the sole judge of fact and of law," but this has not always been the case.

Until the year 1896, the two captains decided whether the game should be stopped, or allowed to continue. Such a system, dependent solely on the goodwill of the two captains had its problems – slow to administer and open to dispute – and in 1885 the RFU laid down that two umpires and a referee be appointed to control the game. These officials however, could only adjudicate, the captains of the teams still had, as in cricket, to appeal for a decision. Ironically, it was this system which produced the law – that of advantage – which most distinguishes rugby football from other games, for no captain would appeal for a stoppage if his team had gained an advantage from his opponent's mistake.

By 1889 the umpires had become touch judges, and by 1896 the practice of appeals was done away with and the phrase "The referee shall be the sole judge of fact" was inserted in the Laws.

The formation of a League structure in English Rugby, back in 1987, brought about the introduction of Society appointed neutral touch judges. The majority of these were older referees and they were soon given the authority to stop the game if they saw any player committing an offence under law 26, which covers foul play. The touch judge should bring such offences to the attention of the referee by raising his flag to the horizontal and pointing it in field. When the referee notices the signal, he is obliged to stop the game and get a report on the incident from the touch judge. Although the referee might ask the touch judge for an opinion, it is the referee who decides the action to take and how to restart the game. Officials working in teams of three is thought by the RFU to be the way forward and methods are being devised so that more information can be given to the referee by his two touch judges.

During the 1996/97 Season the RFU tried wiring up the referee and the senior touch judge, but the experiment was abandoned. Perhaps the next experiment will be an extra official, Cricket style, with slow motion play back video equipment. Watch this space!

FIT TO REF?

There has been much discussion on what makes a good referee. In my opinion, and in the simplest of terms, I believe that the better referees are good 'man managers', who are consistent and fair; they should know the law and be fit enough to get themselves in the correct position to apply it.

Fitness has become more crucial since the players became professional and considerably fitter. At the same time recent law changes have been introduced providing faster and more free flowing games.

In its efforts to keep the ball 'alive' the law makes it very clear what the tackler or tackled player may or may not do whilst on the floor. It is also very clear what the supporting players may or may not do, when approaching a tackle situation. The highest standards are essential when refereeing these specific laws if the game is to develop into the fast, free flowing game desired by all. In order to achieve this, today's referee must be capable of getting to every breakdown as soon as, if not before, the supporting players. That is to say, **today's referee should be covering the field in his particular standard of game at the same rate as the open side flankers.**

When a referee is ten or fifteen yards away from a breakdown it is obviously more difficult for him to see what is happening, but even if from this distance he is able to pick out the FIRST OFFENDER, he will find that being those extra few yards off the pace of the game will severely erode his credibility among the players.

This is recognised by the RFU and all senior referees are obliged to take a fitness test twice each season and failure to achieve the required standard would mean automatic downgrading.

REFEREE POSITIONING

When talking about referee positioning we are getting into the realms of the 'ART' of refereeing as opposed to the pure science of getting the law correct. Therefore there is no right or wrong and every situation will be different. The referee should always strive to position himself where he feels he can get the best view of what is going on without getting in the way of the players. Finding oneself standing between the scrumhalf and the flyhalf at the time the ball emerges from the scrummage, ruck, or maul, is a cardinal sin for a referee. Good positioning and correct lines of running give the impression that the referee is calm, relaxed and in full control. Poor positioning gives the impression that the referee is flustered, nervous and lacking in confidence.

In open play situations the referee will attempt to keep as close to the ball as he can without getting in the way. Achievement of this will be largely dependent on his level of fitness, which for the modern game needs to be of a very high standard. However, even the fittest of referees will not be able to stay close to the ball as it is passed along the threequarter line, so on such occasions the referee should change his line of running, with a view to staying level with the ball. In this way, by sacrificing being close to the ball, for being level with it, he will be able to make accurate decisions relating to forward passes and he will arrive at the in-goal area at the same time, if not before the ball.

At scrummages, rucks and mauls, most referees first take a close look to establish who has possession of the ball and then take up a position on the back corner. If you imagine lines drawn parallel with the goal lines and the touch lines, so that they just embrace all of the players involved in the scrummage, ruck, or maul, you will contain them in a box. One of the four corners of such an imaginary box is usually the favoured position for the referee. When stood in this position, level with the back player, he can never be in the way of the pass from scrumhalf to flyhalf, which must not go forward and he will be able to see all of the important things that might go on.

The better referees usually choose to stand on one of the two corners of the team that are in possession. In this way they can see the ball, all of the players involved in the scrummage, ruck, or maul and MOST IMPORTANTLY, all of the defending threequarters, who do, after all, have most to gain by cheating. The only players that will be out of the direct sight of the referee are the backs of the side in possession and they have absolutely nothing to gain by advancing in front of their off-side line. The players like to see off-side refereed strictly and consistently so that they all get the space they are entitled to in which to play.

Believe it or not, players can be quite forgiving towards the referee if he misses the odd knock-on etc., but they are equally unforgiving if a legitimate try is disallowed. For this reason whenever play approaches an in-goal area, the better referees take up positions on the goal line side, or make sure that they can get into the in-goal area before the ball carrier. A referee who gets deep into the in-goal and is therefore looking back at the players, should never be unsighted when the ball is touched down.

A lot of thought goes into the subject of lines of running and positioning by referee societies, but as mentioned before, it is an art and not a science, so there is no single solution. The better referees use their experience to pick the best position and then asses the 'percentage options'. By this I mean, they try to anticipate what is most likely to happen next, so that they are ready and prepared to move on when it happens. As the title "percentage option" suggests there is clearly an element of chance related and success will depend on the ability of the individual referee to "read the game". The clues that are available are such things as: Position on the field. Are the ball carriers attacking or defending? The weather conditions – is it raining, windy or is the sun shining. The score and the amount of time remaining. The position taken up by the players, especially the threequarters. The size and shape of the pitch. Any one or a combination of such things can give an experienced referee a very good idea of what tactic is most likely to be tried next by the team in possession.

REFEREE TRAINING AND DEVELOPMENT

County Referee Societies have been responsible for the recruitment, training and appointing of referees within their own individual areas for many years. Dependent largely on local talent, knowledge and management skills, the standards of training in particular have varied enormously. Many were very good, others adequate, but some were very poor or non-existent.

When appointed to the position of National Referee Development Officer, about 3 years ago, Steve Griffiths was very quick to recognise this as a weakness and started to put together training packages. As a result of his foresight the RFU now have a complete set of structured training packages that embrace the needs of all refereeing categories – (see pyramid diagram opposite).

Through the Referee Training Officer in each County Society, the RFU are able to offer support and training for everyone, from a father helping out with the mini and midi rugby on Sunday mornings, through to the senior referees taking first team games on Saturday afternoons.

THE PILKINGTON AWARD LEVEL 1.

A course for people wishing to referee mini of midi rugby, which is played according to the rules of the continuum, by children under the age of 13 years. Candidates are expected to attend a series of theory sessions – referee 5 games and pass a test on the laws of the game. Successful candidates who are able to show they can handle a game safely, are presented with the Pilkington Award Certificate and a badge.

THE TEACHERS CERTIFICATE.

Aimed at all teachers who are required to referee school matches, whether it be in practices, or in inter-school games, at any level. Teachers attend a one day course comprising theory sessions, a knowledge questionnaire and a practical. Candidates who achieve the appropriate score on the questionnaire and show that they are able to referee safely, receive the Teachers Referee Certificate.

THE CLUB REFEREE CERTIFICATE.

Newly launched in 1996 to help people who enjoy refereeing at their own club when required, but have no desire to become a member of a Referee Society. Structured in a very similar way to the Teacher's Certificate, it compromises a one day course with theory sessions, a questionnaire and a practical. Successful candidates receive a Certificate of Competence.

All the above courses pay particular attention to the use of safe practices on the rugby field, especially in rucks, mauls and the scrummage.

THE PILKINGTON AWARD LEVEL 2.

Those who successfully gain one of the lower awards, are encouraged to move on and take this course, which is aimed at those who wish to referee 15-a-side rugby for players between the ages of 13 and 19 years. Candidates have to attend monthly theory sessions, run touch at an adult game, take a law examination and referee a minimum of five games.

B & C GRADE TRAINING AND DEVELOPMENT.

These courses are run by the County Societies for their members, who are expected to attend monthly theory sessions. At certain times in the season they will be able to take a law examination to test their knowledge. Failure to pass this Society examination would mean that they would not be eligible to progress on to the upper grades. However passing the examination will not mean automatic upgrading. Progress to the higher grades is mostly dependent on their performances on the field. Much of the training time is devoted to man management skills and positioning in game situations.

Those referees who progress through the County Society system, to the RFU panel are largely looked after by Twickenham directly. This is done by running week-end seminars, monthly written bulletins and individual tuition by the RFU panel development squad. The National Development Squad is the responsibility of the International Referee Selection Committee, which is made up of eight experienced ex-referees. This Committee enlisted six additional referee coaches who were paired off with the top ten referees to provide a one to one coaching situation. In this way the selectors and coaches all work together and share their knowledge for the referee's benefit. It is this group that set up the meetings with the First and Second Division clubs, encouraging frank exchanges of view between the referees, selectors, referee coaches and the club coaches, on the aspects of the game causing most concern. One would not claim that things are perfect, but with referees now talking with club coaches in this way, we must be heading in the correct direction.

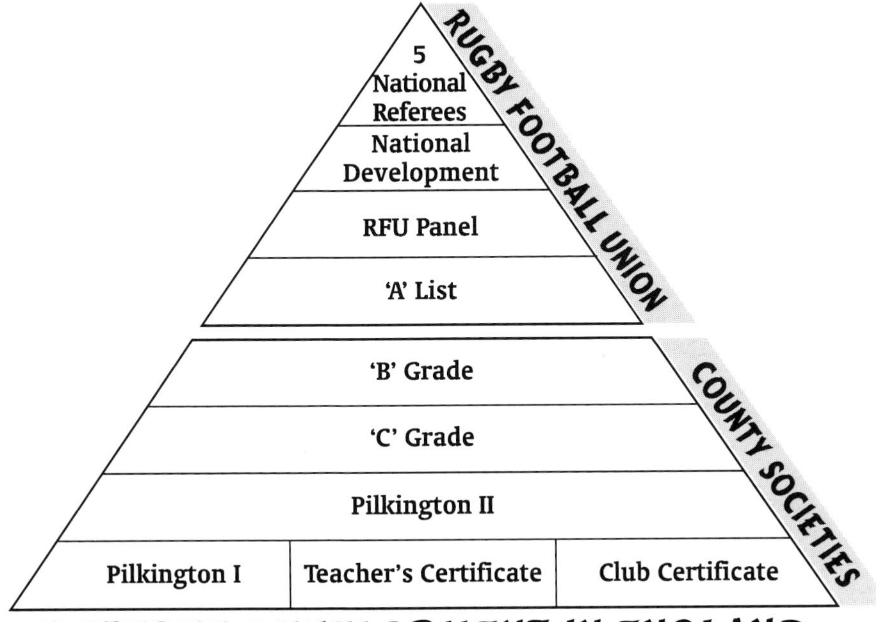

REFEREE DEVELOPMENT IN ENGLAND

REFEREE DECISION MAKING

In most sports, the prime objective of the referee is to apply the rules of the game, with a view to gaining a fair result. If this philosophy was applied in rugby football, we might achieve a fair result, but there would be little chance of producing a game that was worth playing or watching. By comparison our game is very complicated. For example, in soccer, when the ball crosses the plane of the touch line it is always judged to be in touch. Not so in rugby football! In our game it is possible for a player to hold the ball at least one metre OUT of the field of play and yet keep it IN, or hold the ball at least one metre IN the field of play, for it to be judged OUT. If you are confused, then I rest my case. The decision on each occasion is dependent on the position of the players feet in relationship to the touch line. Even in such a simple example the situation is not black or white, and the same applies to the scrummage, ruck, maul, lineout and off-side, only more so.

In view of the complexity of the laws of rugby and because there are so many potential offences that might be committed, the better referees apply their minds to looking for reasons NOT to blow the whistle. On occasions when the letter of the law is strictly applied the game deteriorates into a series of whistles followed by the inevitable scrummage, penalty, or free kick and there is no continuity or open play. To prevent this happening the referees PRIORITISE their decisions, separating the important offences from the less important, bringing refereeing into the realms of an art form. The better referees, will consider such things as:

- Is any player in danger?
- Can advantage be played?
- What was the intent of the offender?
- Did the offence affect the run of play?
- Which was the first offence?

Whenever the referee thinks that continued play would endanger a player he should always stop the game immediately. The advantage law in such situations should not be a consideration. At other times it usually can be applied, providing valuable thinking time for the referee.

The intention of a player's action can often determine whether the game is stopped or not. Did he deliberately fall over the ball or did he trip over a player on the ground? Did he deliberately hold onto the ball to prevent the opposition taking a free kick quickly or did he genuinely think the decision had been given his way?

On other occasions, the offence might be thought to be of no great consequence to the run of the game. Two second row players, standing at the front of the line, begin to push and shove each other while the ball has been thrown to the back. A wing forward who breaks from the scrummage before the ball is out, realises his mistake and joins back on. Both are clear cut penalty offences, but should the game be stopped?

Finally, it is also very important that the referee penalises the first offence. A player jumping across the lineout should not be penalised if he was following a ball that had not been thrown in straight in the first instance. Neither should the tackled player be penalised for not releasing the ball if he himself has not been released by the tackler. It is all rather complicated, but the better referees manage to prioritise the important decisions and then referee them fairly and consistently.

THE REFEREE ADVISOR

Previously known as Assessors, the Referee Advisors are provided by County Referee Societies with a view to helping referees reach their full potential. These people are usually retired referees and they are appointed to watch games of rugby so that they can report back to the referee's society on his performance.

The objective is to help the referee to manage his next game better than the one watched on that day and to report accurately to his Society. Most advisors will seek to talk directly to the referee at some convenient time after each match. The advisor's conduct during such discussions is crucial remembering that most referees are still doing it for pleasure.

Like most people they will not like criticism, but in most cases will accept constructive criticism when tactfully presented. The referee will not want to be told that he missed a blatant knock-on prior to the match winning try. He will have already been told that by a number of players, coaches and spectators before he could get to the bar. What he does want to know, is why he failed to see it, when everyone else did.

The advisor should talk to the referee about why he went wrong, rather than what he did wrong. This may relate to positioning, or why he set off to run too late, but whatever it is he will not recognise he is doing it, otherwise he would have corrected it himself. A discussion covering perhaps three or four main areas of concern enables the referee to return home a wiser man with the experience of his advisor added to his own.

The advisor fills in a report which is returned to the referee's home Society. The report requires a description of the game itself and an assessment of how the referee managed it. Further detailed breakdowns are given on the referee's control of the scrummage, lineout, law 18 (tackle), ruck and maul, advantage and open play. Finally reports are also given on the referee's communication skills, his fitness and positioning. These reports are all logged by the home societies who gain a very good indication of the progress made by individual referees and their training needs.

REFEREE SIGNALS

Referees have adopted hand signals as an aid to the communication between themselves, the players and the spectators. The signals come in two basic groups, PRIMARY and SECONDARY.

Primary Signals relate to the award the referee has made to the non-offending side and their adoption is strongly recommended by the RFU. There are five primary signals given to indicate the following: a TRY, PENALTY, FREE-KICK, SCRUMMAGE and ADVANTAGE. With the exception of advantage the referee would stop the game by blowing his whistle and then use one of the five primary signals to indicate who will restart the game and how.

For penalty-kicks and free-kicks the better referees will signal clearly and quickly, so that the non-offending team can take advantage by taking the kick quickly if they wish. The advantage signal is the only signal that is not preceded with a whistle. This is used when the referee spots an infringement but chooses not to stop the game, as the non-offending team have an opportunity to gain an advantage by playing on.

Secondary signals usually follow primary signals and are used to explain the reason for making an award. Referees are encouraged to adopt the use of secondary signals, but they are not compulsory. Perhaps a couple of examples would best demonstrate the correct procedure:

A) Referee spots a knock-on from which the non-offending team can gain no advantage.

- He blows his whistle to stop play.
- He moves to the place where the knock-on occurred.
- He gives the primary signal for a scrum (outstretched arm parallel to the ground pointing to the side with the right to put the ball in).
- He gives the secondary signal for a knock-on (one hand above the head tapped by the other hand)

B) Referee spots a hooker winning the ball unfairly by having his boot raised, before the ball enters the scrum.

- He blows his whistle to stop play
- He gives the primary signal for a free-kick (upper arm horizontal, fore- arm raised vertically pointing in the direction of the non-offending side)
- He gives the secondary signal for boot-up (foot raised and heel tapped by hand).

In this way the players and spectators should all know why the game was stopped as well as how, where and by whom it is to be restarted.

Basically the Primary signals are used by the referee to indicate who has been awarded a try, scrum, free-kick, penalty, or advantage and the Secondary signals follow to explain why the awards were given. It should be stressed, that the use of signals is not compulsory and many referees choose not to use all of them. The referees priority will be to get the decision right and then to ensure that the players know what he has decided. This he might do by talking to them. If the explanation is accompanied by the appropriate signal this is a bonus that is probably more appreciated by the isolated players such as the full-back, and the spectators.

There are many referees who do not agree with the signal for advantage being used. They would argue that for a side to know that a failure to gain an advantage will still result in a penalty kick, acts as an inducement to be more adventurous than they would have been otherwise.

An interesting new development is the increased participation of the appointed touch judges, now that the officials are encouraged to act as a team of three. When you next go to a First, or Second Division game, spend a little time watching a touch judge and you will notice him making all sorts of gestures with his hands. These are signals to the referee on the field, giving him additional information, gained from a different view point. Although working in teams of three is definitely encouraged by the RFU, it is still early days and the signals given by individual touch judges vary tremendously as they have not yet been formalised.

A SELECTION OF SECONDARY SIGNALS
KNOCK-ON
NOT RELEASING THE BALL
LIFTING IN THE LINEOUT
HIGH TACKLE
CLOSING THE GAP IN A LINEOUT
OBSTRUCTING/ CROSSING
PUNCHING

TIME KEEPING

The referee is the sole judge of time, although I expect it will not be long before the likes of Murdoch and Packer will be dictating when matches should start, finish and how many 'timeouts' there should be to allow for advertisements. The thin end of that wedge has been inserted this Season with the introduction of ten minute breaks for half time and players leaving the field.

Presently the game consists of two halves of forty minutes duration, with a break for half-time to allow the players to change ends and prepare for the second half. Once the game has started the referee should add on time for delays in the half of the match in which the delay occurs. To assist in accurate timing, most referees use a stop-watch, backed up by a second time-piece.

When a player is injured the referee can allow a stoppage of up to one minute for treatment, unless a longer period is necessary to remove the player or to give essential treatment on the playing area. He should not allow time if he believes that a player is feigning injury. When the ball is dead, time can be allowed for a player to replace or repair a torn jersey or shorts, etc. Some of the longest delays (and often the most blatant time-wasting) occur when a player takes the option of kicking at goal. Referees are instructed to add on any time taken in excess of 40 seconds from the time the player indicates his intention to kick at goal. This applies whether or not the referee considers the delay to be 'undue delay' on the part of the kicker.

When a period of forty minutes has expired the referee can only blow for time when the ball is dead. However, if the ball next becomes dead as a result of one team scoring a try, that team should be allowed to take the conversion kick and if the ball becomes dead as a result of a fair catch, free-kick or penalty kick the game should continue. As there is no limit to the number of penalties or free kicks that a referee can award after forty minutes has expired, the game can often be extended for a considerable length of time.

The referee has the power to declare no-side before time has expired, if in his opinion the full time cannot be played, or the continuance of play would be dangerous. If a league game is stopped because of weather conditions the time of the abandonment becomes crucial. If more than 60 minutes of rugby has been played then the score at the time of abandonment becomes the match result, and if less than 60 minutes is played the two teams should play again within seven days. The outcome of a game that is stopped for any reason other than weather conditions will be determined by the organising committee of the league concerned.

During the 1995/96 seasons the RFU introduced official timekeepers for first division games and they assumed sole responsibility for the time keeping of each game. Sitting at the side of the pitch they ran a stop watch (starting and stopping it at the appropriate times) and blew loud hooters to end each half.

Early in the 1996/97 Season the clubs were all asked to return the official timekeeping equipment and timekeepers ceased to be appointed. There was no official explanation offered, but I do believe that the RFU were finding it difficult to appoint referee advisers and timekeepers to all games in the first four Divisions.

DISCIPLINE

For general matters of discipline the RFU delegates its authority to the constituent bodies, of which there are 32 in England. Each of these constituent bodies must provide a disciplinary committee who have the power to expel or inflict other appropriate punishment to any club or individual infringing the laws of the game.

Most of the County Rugby Football Unions have a disciplinary committee made up of a chairman, secretary and 8 panel members. The panel members being elected representatives from clubs who play within the county, of which a minimum of 4 must be present to form the committee. A member of the local Referees Society is usually invited to attend every disciplinary committee meeting, but with the possible exception of being asked for guidance on a particular point of law, he would be there solely for the purpose of observing, in order to report back to his Society.

Following the ordering-off of a player, the referee should write a report and send copies to his own Society, the Constituent Body where the game was played and the Constituent Body of the player's team (these might be the same). This should be done within 48 hours. The Club Secretary should also supply the name and address of any player who has been ordered off, to his Constituent Body within the same 48 hours. It is then the responsibility of the Constituent Body where the game was played to organise a disciplinary hearing within 14 days.

The referee, and the player ordered off, are given notice of the hearing, which is accompanied by a copy of the Referee's Report. The player who has been ordered off is entitled to be represented by one person of his choice and his club may be represented by one person of its choice, in addition to Officers or members of the club.

The proceedings within the hearing are quite formal, starting with the reading of the referee's report, followed by the player's statement. Although witnesses can be called in, any further evidence can only be put forward in clarification of the referee's report. The disciplinary committee are obliged to follow the letter of the law, which states "The referee is the sole judge of fact and of law". A club official can speak up as a character reference for the player, after which all parties are asked to leave the room while the committee members make their decision. If guilty, the player is asked to pay the administration costs of the meeting and given a sentence in accordance to RFU guidelines.

Recently a player who was ordered-off was not allowed to take part in training or playing rugby football until after his hearing, but such mandatory suspensions have now been abolished. It is thought that in some cases having to leave the field may be sufficient punishment. This however, does not stop the clubs from suspending their own player following an ordering off, as clubs are encouraged to take more responsibility in this area. Any actions they take themselves will be taken into consideration by the disciplinary committee when they meet. Players are allowed to appeal against any penalty they get, but have to pay a fee in advance, which would not be returned if they were unsuccessful. This has been introduced to deter frivolous appeals. For players under the age of 17 years, the case should be dealt with by the club and the action taken reported to the constitutional body. In the 1996/97 season a Special Disciplinary Committee was formed to cover hearings related to players of clubs playing in Courage Leagues 1, 2 & 3, who were either registered or contracted. All other players being dealt with by the Constituent Body Disciplinary Committee as previously.

This means that a player playing for a League 1, 2, or 3 Club who is neither registered nor contracted, (for example some third or fourth team players,) will continue to be dealt with by the Constituent Body. It is the status of the player and not the match in which he is playing which determines where his case is heard. A registered player of a League 1 Club ordered off in a friendly would therefore appear before the Special Disciplinary Committee.

Referee reports relating to the ordering off of players in this special category should be sent directly to the RFU at Twickenham. Club secretaries of Clubs playing in Leagues 1 to 3 when fulfilling the obligation to report players who are ordered off to their Constituent Bodies, should also send a copy to the RFU at Twickenham.

The Special Disciplinary Committee has been established so that the hearings of the players who fall into the Special category can be dealt with more quickly and by senior members of the RFU, rather than the many well-meaning amateurs we have throughout the Counties. For it is in these three leagues that the majority of International and professional players are playing and their livelihoods could well be directly effected by the outcome of such meetings.

The International Board has decided that video evidence is admissible, but that it should be viewed following the completion of all oral evidence. On occasions when a club wish to show video evidence

the secretary of the disciplinary committee must be notified in advance and the club are required to produce and install the necessary equipment. Should the Disciplinary Committee decide to use video evidence then they should notify the player to whom the report related and provide the required equipment.

The introduction of a new soccer style card system in the 1995/96 season was not at first well received. The controversy was mainly caused, because the system allowed for the totting up of yellow cards from one game to another. A player shown two yellow cards in any one season, even if the games are 30 weeks apart, would be ordered off on the second showing. At the beginning of the 1996/97 season there was a new law bulletin that did away with the totting-up of yellow cards and extended the system to cover all games at all levels.

Following a case resulting in the imprisonment of a player, the RFU have advised referees to consider the ordering off of a player as a first resort. Many referees in the past have felt that they should try and keep players on the field and only order them off as a last resort.

The recommended penalty suspensions for foul play are:

- PUNCHING . . . . . . 30 DAYS
- KICKING or RAKING . . 60 DAYS
- UNFAIR USE OF A BOOT 60 DAYS
- HEAD BUTTING or ASSAULT . . . . . . 60 DAYS
- ABUSE OF MATCH OFFICIAL . . . . 120 DAYS
- STRIKING OF MATCH OFFICIAL . . . . . . BAN FOR LIFE

RUGBY LAWS LABORATORY

Law changes are made by the International Rugby Football Board, who meet to discuss the merits of proposals put forward by member countries. Those that are thought to be an improvement are then ratified and become law. During recent seasons a number of amendments and notes of explanation have been necessary within weeks of the law books being distributed, causing many people to believe that the system requires improvement. To this end, the Laws Advisory Panel and Cambridge University, have established a Rugby Laws Laboratory at Cambridge, who's aim is to extensively try out and evaluate future proposed law changes before they become law. This is one of the better ideas to have come from the southern hemisphere.

Cambridge has been chosen for this exercise because fourteen of the colleges play an internal competition between October and February each year. As such a competition is self-contained, it is possible to advise all players and referees of the experimental laws and conduct the games accordingly. This allows a great deal of information to be gathered very quickly, as a large number of games are played by the colleges in a short space of time. The players are also young, intelligent and ready to adapt to the changes and use them. Such a system, where all of the participants are readily available, even allows for the luxury of an interim evaluation, and amendments at the half way stage.

During the 1996/97 season a new set of experimental laws were evaluated, with a view to achieving some of the following objectives:

- To reduce the amount of aimless kicking and to improve the quality of kicking.
- To encourage tackled players to release the ball away from the body with less fear of opposition players taking the ball.
- To reduce the amount of "pulling down" in the scrummage.
- To prevent the eighth player in the scrummage from binding outside the flank forwards and reducing midfield space.
- To ensure that the ball is moved quickly from rucks.
- To ensure that the effect of a minor misdemeanour is not penalised too heavily.
- To ensure that there are not repeated penalties for players not retiring, in situations where it is not possible to retire.
- To encourage players not to concede penalties and to focus on legal defence. At the same time, not to allow technical offences outside the 10 metre line to have an effect on the score and to reward quality goal kicking.

The above is an insight to the way the minds of the Law makers are thinking. It will be interesting to see what changes are made in the future, as a direct result of the above experiments.

ANSWER TO QUESTION ON PAGE 47

A player who has his feet in touch can score as try by placing downward pressure on a ball that is lying in the goal area. Only if he picks the ball up is it deemed to be in touch

THE TOUCH JUDGE

For years the job of running the line was done by an injured player, an elder-statesman of the club, or even by a lone spectator who foolishly showed up before the kick-off time. In the early seventies, when I was playing for Leicester, the touch was always run by club coach Chalkie White. When the league structure was introduced in 1987, the Senior clubs were quick to complain about the standard of touch judging, and although they all believed that their own touch judges were perfectly fair and competent, they did not feel the same way about those provided by their opponents. This led to the introduction of RFU appointed touch judges for all games at divisions 4 and above. Today the officials are very much a team of three, trained to work together with the referee as the leader. Before each game the touch judges are briefed by the referee, who explains his requirements of them. Their most obvious priority is to judge if the ball is in touch, but there are now numerous other ways in which they are expected to assist the referee.

The senior touch judge is often asked to brief the ball boys before the game. He would instruct them not to field a ball that was lying in touch if it could be used for a quick throw by a player and not to throw a spare ball directly to a player, but instead to place it on the ground at the feet of the touch judge on the line of touch. This is done so that the ball boys are never seen to take away or give an advantage to either side.

When the ball has gone into touch the touch judge should raise his flag and run to the line of touch, but should not raise his other arm to indicate who should throw-in, until after the right to take a quick throw has gone (when a line out is formed, or the ball touched by a spectator). In this way the referee gains additional information, helping him to judge if a quick throw is legal or not.

Generally throughout the game the three officials attempt to "triangulate" on the ball. For instance if the ball emerging from a scrum is moved towards touch judge 'A' he will lead and run along his line ahead of the ball. Touch judge 'B' should dwell level with the place the scrum took place long enough to ensure that all players are proceeding to the next play and not indulging in illegal activities. If from the same scrum the ball is played towards touch judge 'B' it is he who should run foreward along the line ahead of play, and touch judge 'A' should stay. The referee who makes up the third point of the triangle will keep close to the ball. (see diagrams opposite)

Various other aids are offered for the assistance of the referee, such as marking the off-side line for the side not in possession at lineouts and penalty kicks etc., and indicating whether a try has been scored in a difficult corner-flag situation.

Qualified touch judges are also instructed to signal misconduct and foul play by raising their flag parallel to the ground and pointing across the pitch. If this is done the referee will stop the game while the touch judge reports a player, the offence and his recommended action.

The RFU are very keen on the officials working as teams of three. Experiments were conducted where the referee was wired up to his touch judges for sound, but these were discontinued early in the 1996/97 season. No official explanation was given by the RFU, but it is thought that the referees found the system to be too distracting.

MOVEMENT OF TOUCH JUDGES

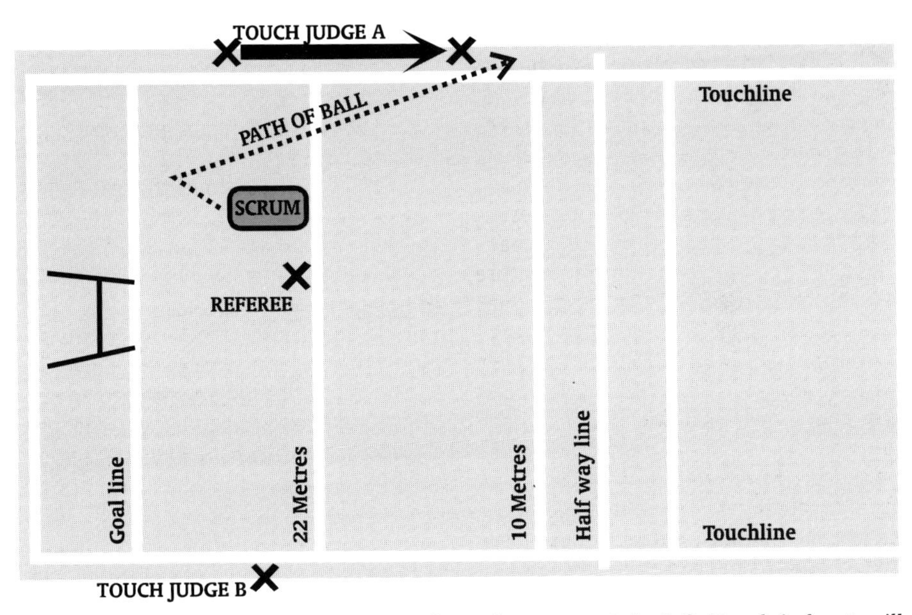

In the top diagram the ball emerges from the scrum to the left. Touch judge A will advance with the ball, whilst touch judge B dwells at the line of scrummage. If, in the same situation, the ball moves to the right, as shown below, the roles are reversed

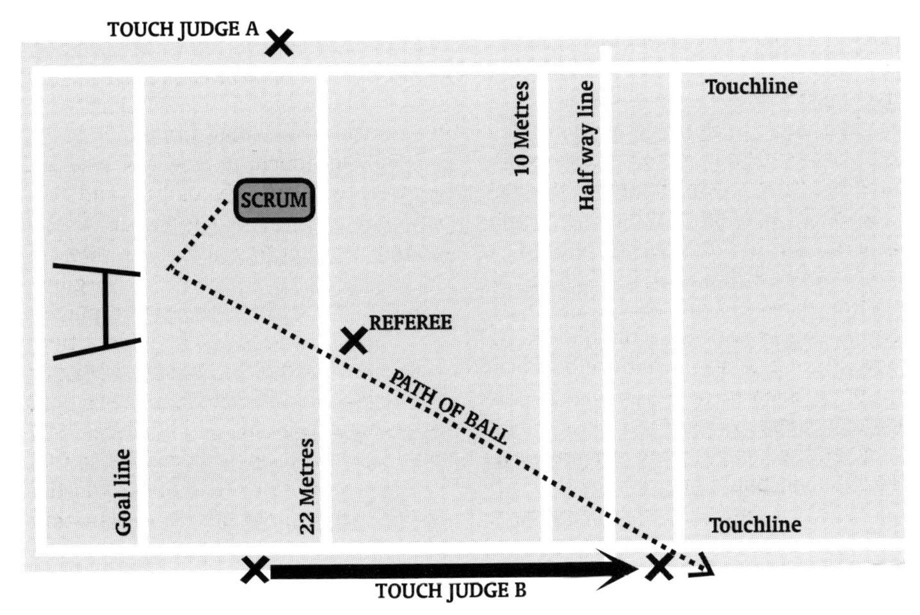

1996/97 NEW LAWS REVIEWED

Ever since the Rugby Football Union was formed in 1871, we have been adding and amending laws with a view to obtaining the ultimate ball game. Each Laws Committee in turn making their seasonal contribution. In 1996 they had a field day and introduced the largest number and the most significant changes made to date; the most revolutionary being, the introduction of professionalism.

Those wishing to be successful had to adapt a more businesslike approach and the expectancy of everyone increased. Players are expected to be bigger, stronger, fitter and more skilful. Coaches are expected to recruit, train and select, successful teams. Administrators are expected to provide better facilities and the money. Referees are expected to be perfect.

The "spirit" of the game is now being severely tested and the outcome will be in the hands of the players, coaches and referees. Unfortunately the early signs are not too good, as the "professional foul", or deliberate repeated infringements, have flourished during the season. The referees responded in the best way they knew how, by awarding penalty tries. This was done when, but for a series of illegal actions close to the goal line, a try would probably have been scored. As a result referees have awarded 25 penalty tries in the first division this season, compared to 8 last year.

Relating to play on the field there were over 40 changes made to the laws. Some were minor amendments which simply clarified existing laws, but the more significant changes were introduced to achieve the following key objectives:

- TO CREATE MORE SPACE IN WHICH TO RUN WITH THE BALL.
- TO ENCOURAGE PLAYERS TO KEEP THE BALL ALIVE.
- TO PROVIDE A SAFER ENVIRONMENT FOR THE PLAYERS.

Lack of space was a particular problem around the perimeter of the set scrummage. It had become common practice for teams to "drop-off" back row forwards while the ball was still in the scrummage, in order to form a defensive wall. Backed up by the scrum-half they had successfully managed to "snuff-out" most opposition moves close to the scrummage. The new law now requires each team to have eight players bound into the scrummage for its duration and for the scrum-half to remain close to the scrummage. Instead of running into a wall of defenders, the ball carrier is now more likely to confront a one-to-one situation; which increases the possibilities of him crossing the gain line, or even making the breakthrough.

Keeping the ball alive is a bigger problem, as one can never realistically expect co-operation from the side who do not have possession. However, attempts were made by changing the laws relating to, the tackle, quickly taken penalties, drop outs and lineouts.

In the tackle situation the new law made it very clear that the onus was in the first instance on the tackling player, to allow the tackled player his right to pass, place, or release the ball. When releasing the ball the players were encouraged to move it away from their own bodies, making it easier for the arriving players on their feet to pick up. Failure to comply with this put the tackled player at risk of being penalised for holding the ball. Referees have now set priorities for the tackle situation and will look to penalise the tackler first, the ball carrier second and arriving players, who do not stay on their feet, third. When this is refereed consistently and well, it does help to keep the ball alive.

Probably the biggest contributor towards keeping the ball alive has been the quickly taken penalty, because the new law dictates that the kickers do not have to wait for their own players to get back on-side; Opponents who have not retired 10 metres cannot be played on-side by any action of the team taking the kick and the kick itself can be taken from within a 1 metre channel of the referee's mark.

Unfortunately many referees have been so keen to enter into the spirit of this new law, that they are allowing kicks to be taken in front of the mark. This is unfair to the defending team because they concede the stolen metres and more importantly loose the time that their opponents would have taken, getting the ball back to the correct position, behind the mark. Never-the-less, it has been the catalyst for much of the additional, exciting running rugby that we have seen throughout the season.

The law covering 22 metre drop outs has also helped to keep the game alive in two ways. Firstly, the defending team can take the kick quickly without having to wait for team mates to get back on-side, just as one can for penalties and free kicks. Secondly, when the ball is kicked dead into touch in goal, or over the dead ball line (with the exception of kicks at goal) the defending team are offered the 22 drop out, or a scrummage at the place where the ball was kicked. This option to scrummage has been the popular choice for defending teams, as they are more likely to retain possession and the mark for the scrummage is frequently many metres in front of their 22 metre line. This new law has stopped players deliberately kicking the ball dead.

In the lineout jumpers can now legally be supported provided they leave the ground under their own steam. As a result they are achieving greater heights and more importantly they are able to "hover" when at their peak. The players throwing in the ball, are now waiting until their jumper is in "hover mode" and then throwing the ball directly to him. This does keep the ball alive, because the team throwing in are now virtually assured of possession, in the same way as they are at the set scrummage. But is this a fair contest?

Improving safety for the players has been addressed by changing the laws relating to replacements and players dress. Being allowed to name a squad of 21 players for each game, five of which must be front row specialists, greatly reduces the risk of players continuing to play when not fit, or being asked to play out of position.

On the subject of players dress, the RFU stipulated very clearly exactly what could and what could not be worn, only to be completely ignored by the majority of senior referees. This lack of discipline among the senior ranks has caused problems because it will now be very difficult to persuade a player that he cannot wear a body harness that he has been allowed to wear throughout the previous season.

In the First Division during the 1995-96 season there were 3,878 points scored in total (402 tries – 8 penalty tries), compared to 5,773 (666 tries – 25 penalty tries) in the 1996-97 season. So we have seen 1,895 more points scored in total, including 264 extra tries, which supports the general view that the new laws have improved the game of rugby and that the objectives of the Laws committee have been achieved. Congratulations to them and the near perfect referees.

Statistics provided by Stuart Farmer.

ABOUT THE AUTHOR

Growing up in Devon with an enthusiasm for a wide range of sports, Mike Mortimer discovered rugby at St. John's Teacher Training College, York. Beginning as a wing threequarter, in his second season he moved to the second row, found the position suited him well, and other sports took a back seat.

In 1965 he moved to Leicestershire to teach, with his sights set on a place in the Leicester Tigers team, but in the meantime introduced the Martin High School, Anstey, to rugby. Within three years the school was able to field teams at all age levels, as it still does.

In his personal ambitions Mike found that at 6ft 2in he was deemed too small for a top-level second-row forward, so turned to local club rugby. But after four years, he made another attempt for the Tigers, this time as a tight-head prop. Following some difficult moments in his first matches, Mike established himself as the first choice for this position in 1971, and over the next five seasons made 132 first team appearances, as well as being selected for Leicestershire, Devon, and Midland Counties.

Retiring from the first-class game in 1976, he returned to his local club – Stoneygate – where he continued to play for a further six seasons – as club captain for two of them. By 1982, beginning to feel the knocks, Mike changed tack, and joined the surprisingly competitive world of refereeing, through the Leicestershire Society of Referees. In his search for progress in his new pastime, Mike identified two potential weaknesses. Firstly, despite years of playing rugby, he became aware how limited was his knowledge of the laws of the game, and secondly, by now he was forty years old. To overcome the first problem, he religiously studied one law each day, repeatedly over a two year period, to gain the depth of understanding he required. He is still searching for a solution to the second, which is now bordering on the chronic.

However, within three years he had made the Midland Counties 'B1' list, revisiting as referee the grounds around the country that he had previously been to as a player. After twelve years of refereeing senior rugby, Mike retired and returned to the Leicester Tigers as a selector, as well as a contributor to the club programme. Along with these jobs Mike took on the post of Referee Co-ordinator – responsible for management and hospitality arrangements for referees, touch judges, and advisers at home games.

Since the publication of the first edition of ***Rugby Law Explained,*** Mike has been invited to contribute to Twickenham match programmes, been a speaker at RFU Midland training seminars, and was invited to Malta to update the Maltese RFU on the 1996 law changes.

He remains a full member of the Leicestershire Society of Referees, where he is currently the Training Officer. On Sunday mornings he can still be seen out and about in the Leicestershire clubs, refereeing junior rugby.

Introducti

The first six walks in this book all sta
Harlech – the Bron y Graig Uchaf (upp
to a bus stop. Its location is shown on the map
not to confuse it with the nearby Bron y Graig Isaf (lower) short-stay car park. **The remaining nine walks** are located close to Harlech, with none of their starting points more than a 20 minute drive from the town.

The location of all the walks is indicated on the back cover map, and a summary of the key features and length of all the walks is given in the chart on the inside back cover. The walks vary in length between 2½ miles and 6 miles. All can be managed by a reasonably fit person, but in this area there are, of course, some uphill sections.

The name 'Harlech' is thought to be derived from the term 'beautiful slope'. Walks **2** to **6** take you up the 'slope' to enjoy the outstanding views over a wide sea and an even bigger sky. Sunsets, if you can arrange to be out to see one, will be long remembered. And once on the crest of the 'slope' there are also extensive views in the other directions far to the north and east. Many of the high mountains of the Snowdonia National Park can be seen.

Walks **7** to **15** take you to areas a little further into the countryside around Harlech. The evidence provided by the many standing stones, burial places, homesteads and hut circles makes it certain that the area was first settled many thousands of years ago. And from relatively more recent times there are remains of hillforts and trackways. It is a rich source for anyone interested in ancient history.

For the general countryside lover too the area is exceptional. It is attention-holding landscape. There are so many wonderful rock outcroppings. Oak trees can appear to grow out of the rock faces, and woodland floors have boulders covered with thick green cushions of moss. Mosses are on stone walls and even up tree trunks, sometimes with ferns high up which wave to you in the gentlest of breezes.

Most surprisingly, there are places where you can stand to look around and imagine yourself to be in any time period since the glaciers retreated, because there is no evidence of what man has done since. It is special. Go slowly and quietly, and these walks will give you a taste of this precious area.

Maybe you will want to explore it further.

WALK 1

HARLECH BEACH via THE DUNES

DESCRIPTION This easy 2½ mile walk takes a not-so-well known route through the town's outskirts, has the classic view of the Castle, and uses a sandy path across the dunes to reach a section of the beach much less used than that reached from the popular beach car park.

START The Bron y Graig Uchaf long-stay car park (not to be confused with the Bron y Graig Isaf short-stay car park). See the map on the inside front cover.

1 From the car park go out onto the road. Turn RIGHT along it and go down to the main road and shops. Turn LEFT along the main road and go past the shops. Where the pavement on the right hand side ends, take the signed footpath off to the RIGHT. Go up on to the rocky outcrops on the right to see the view indicator. *This is the place for the classic photographs of the Castle with some of the high Snowdonia mountains in the background.* Go back down to the path and turn RIGHT. Carry on down this path to reach the main (A496) road. Cross it carefully, and at a gap in the railing, go down seven steps and turn RIGHT along a narrow passageway. At the bottom turn LEFT, along a surfaced track. *The mixture of buildings now seen on your left is Coleg Harlech. This is an adult education college which opened in 1927. At its centre is the former house, Wern Fawr, built in 1908 by George Davison, then Managing Director in the U.K. of Kodak. Later, following the purchase of a villa in France, he was persuaded to sell it in 1925 to Cardiff businessman, Henry Gethin Lewis, who donated the property for use as a college for adult students. Created by a few determined people who could see the deficiencies in the formal education system, the college's history makes interesting reading.*

2 After about 300 yards, go RIGHT through a waymarked gate and across the railway – TAKE GREAT CARE!. Then take the waymarked path LEFT along a rough surfaced track. After about 200 yards, where the track curves left, take the clear wide path off to the right, heading more directly to the high dunes and the sea. Follow along this main sandy path. *There are fine views of the Castle behind to the right and opportunities to enjoy the dune flowers.* Go up over the high dunes, and the sea and beach come into view. Explore the beach, of course, but the route of this walk is to turn RIGHT (north) along it. *There are excellent views of some of the Snowdonia mountains from this part of the beach, and, of course, the Lleyn Peninsula.* Go along the beach for about ¾ mile, when the main entrance and exit is reached. It is at a wide gap in a fence safeguarding the dunes, and where there is a high red and white pole. Take the wide sandy track between wire fences. It later becomes surfaced and then joins a metalled road at the beach car park.

3 Continue straight ahead towards the Castle. At the end of this road turn RIGHT, and go through the gate on the right and follow the path parallel to the road. After about 200 yards, where it is joined from the right by a path from the swimming pool, go LEFT across the railway and out on to the main road opposite a letter box. Cross the main road and go up the minor road signed 'Town Centre'. This zig-zags uphill (*there are seats!*) and where the road divides, go LEFT, past the 20% sign. When Harlech's main street is reached, go RIGHT to go back to the car park. There is a pleasant path to the car park off to the LEFT just before the Church entrance. *Look for the rock cannon holes (used in the celebration of important events with gunpowder) as you approach the car park.*

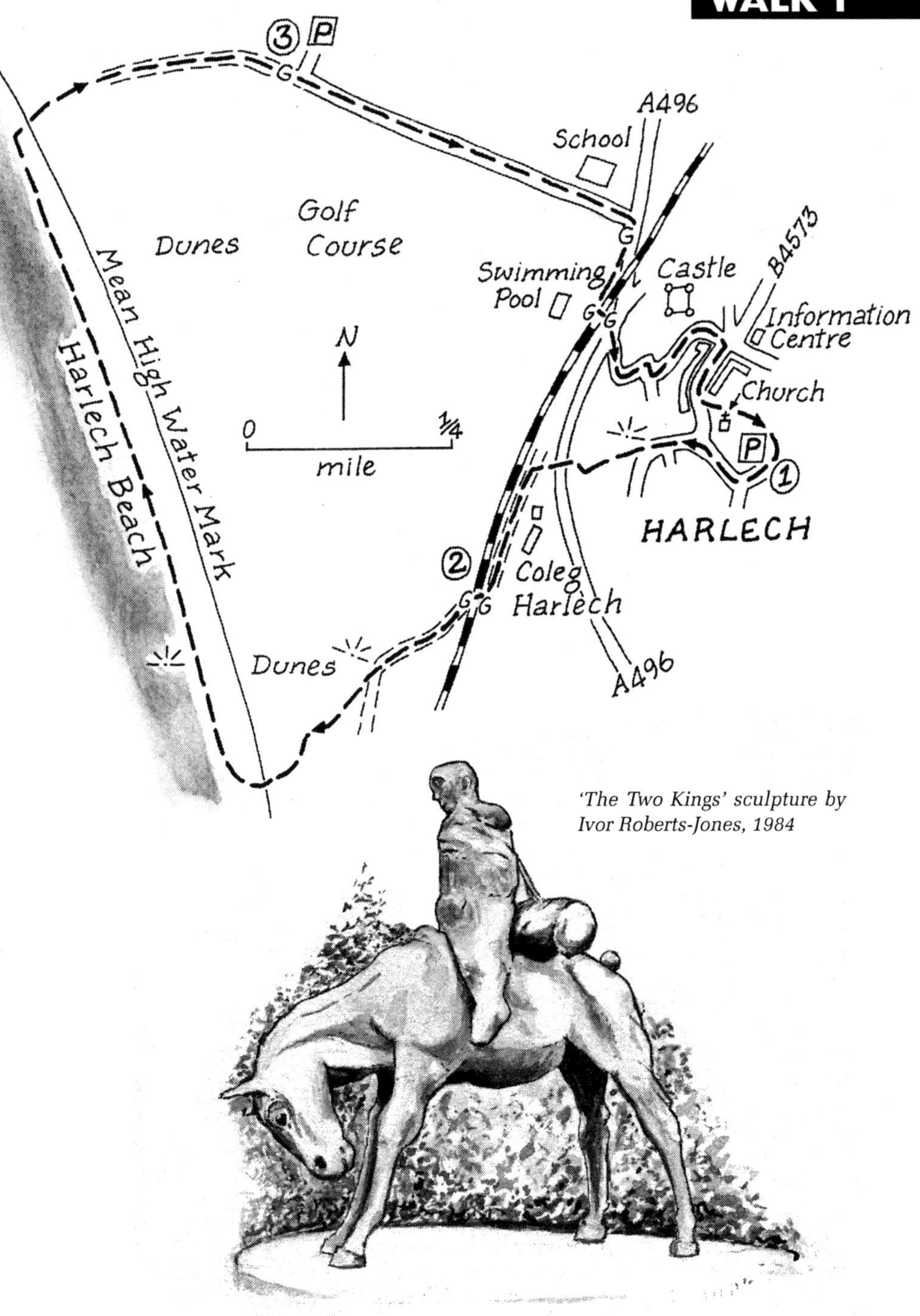

'The Two Kings' sculpture by Ivor Roberts-Jones, 1984

WALK 2

RHINOG VIEW

DESCRIPTION A 2½ mile walk going just over the 'slope' behind Harlech to give fine extensive views of the Rhinog range of mountains, not visible from the town. It passes former farmhouses and barns, and although uphill near the start, the final mile is all downhill with outstanding views along that whole length.
START The Bron y Graig Uchaf long-stay car park (not to be confused with the Bron y Graig Isaf short-stay car park). See the map on the inside front cover.

1 From the car park go out onto the road and turn LEFT. Walk along to the end of the high stone wall on the right. Just beyond the gate to view the duck pond take a narrow signed footpath off RIGHT. When it reaches a road, go RIGHT, and then almost immediately LEFT along another road. Go past a cemetery and keep on ahead along the rough surfaced track. Stay on this track until after passing, on the left, gates to the property Llys Bach. Then take the waymarked path slightly LEFT. This path later emerges at a surfaced parking area near a house. Carry on ahead along a path towards a narrow gap. Go through and ahead to a small gate and then on to a junction of signed paths.

2 Take the path back sharp RIGHT, up into the trees and which follows close to a wall on the right. When the path comes out into the open, leave the wall and zig-zag half-LEFT up the field. *This is steep, but pausing gives a chance to enjoy the fine views.* Towards the top of the field pass along close to the high gorse and natural rock wall on the left and alongside a tree. A waymark post on the wall ahead comes into view. Cross the wall at the post and go ahead as indicated up to a yellow-top-post at a grass track. Go LEFT along it up to a waymark and on to double gates in front of two houses. Go through and ahead along a waymarked walled track between the houses. Stay on this green lane until it ends at an old barn. Pass to the left of the barn over a stile. Carry on up the field (parallel to the long side wall of the barn) and through a gap in the wall ahead. Turn LEFT and through another wall gap. Now go RIGHT, up the field to a swing gate.

3 Go through and LEFT and almost immediately, where the track divides, bear RIGHT up to a gate at Garth Mawr. Go through the gate and stay on the track to reach the house. At the gate to the right of the house, go through and then sharp LEFT to go over a low wall. Go ahead across the field and over a waymarked stile in the wall ahead. Carry on ahead at first, but then work half-RIGHT over to a curving wall. Follow this around with the wall on your left. Near the top of the field, go RIGHT to a gated stile. Go over and ahead, passing to the LEFT of an old building. Keeping ahead in the same direction, cross another stile in the wall ahead. Follow the path ahead through the gorse, across a bridged small stream and out over a stile onto a road. *Here there are fine views across to the Rhinog mountains. They reach about 2,500 feet and provide some fine ridge walking. Elsewhere on these mountains, and if away from the used paths, walking can sometimes be difficult, but nevertheless very rewarding in the enjoyment of the wild beauty and archaeological remains from prehistory to 19th century manganese workings. If you are tempted to get closer to them other walks in the book will take you nearer: Walk **9** is close to Moel Ysgyfarnogod in the north; Walks **14** and **15**, further south, give fine closer views of the three highest tops.*

4 Go RIGHT along the road, staying on it for about ¼ mile to reach a gate and stone step-stile in the wall on your right. Cross the stile and wal;k ahead close to the wall on the right. When the wall veers right, go half-LEFT uphill to cross the wall ahead by the waymarked stile. Carry on ahead in the same direction and, at the crest, aim for the ladder stile now in view in the wall ahead. *There is a strangely positioned, and no doubt now redundant, trig point in this field, to the right over by the wall. The OS map shows it at a height of 258 metres, but it is not at the highest point. Anyway, there are fine views from*

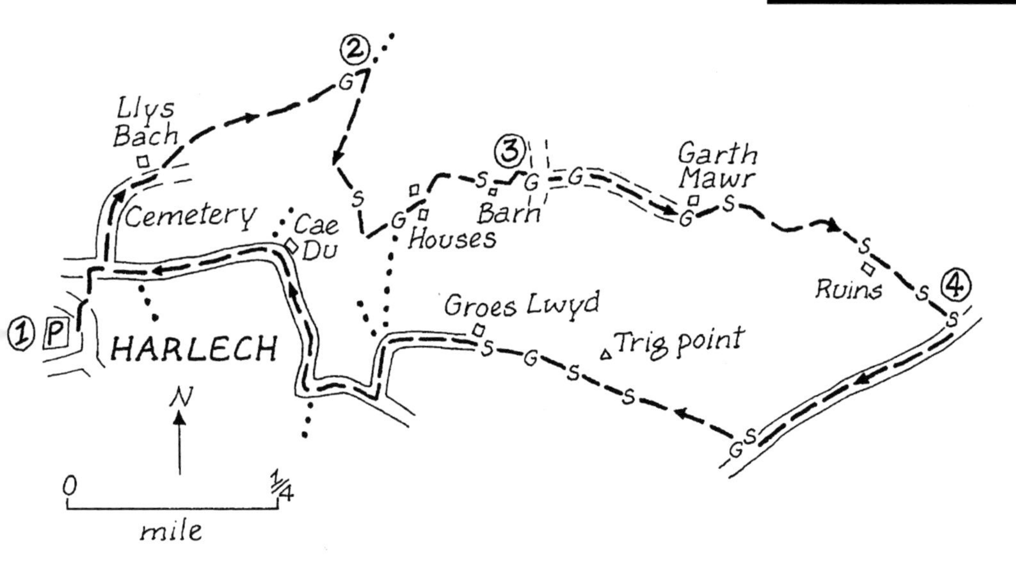

here, and it is certainly worth pausing. Cross the ladder stile and drop straight down to a swing gate. Go through into the walled lane and down over a stile to pass to the left of the house Groes Lwyd. A minor road starts here and can be followed ¾ mile downhill all the way to Harlech, turning right at the T junction

Garth Mawr

WALK 3
FOEL SENIGL

DESCRIPTION This 4 mile walk goes to the top of Foel Senigl, the nearest of the hills behind Harlech. Although only 1000 feet high, its detached position gives wonderful all-round distant views and it is well worth the moderate ascent. As with other walks, the views all along the route will make you want to go slowly.
START The Bron y Graig Uchaf long-stay car park (not to be confused with the Bron y Graig Isaf short-stay car park). See the map on the inside front cover.

1 From the car park go out onto the road and turn LEFT. Walk along to the end of the high stone wall on the right. Just beyond the gate to view the duck pond, take a narrow signed footpath off RIGHT alongside the first house. When it reaches a road, go RIGHT. *After about 100 yards there is an old Scotch Baptist Chapel baptism pool, created in 1841.* Carry on along the road, past the house Cae Du and up past an old barn on the right *(a listed building, with graded slate roof and built, like many in this area, into the hillside slope, usually to give easy access at the back to an upper storage area).* Continue up the road. At a T-junction on the left turn LEFT.

2 Pass a bungalow on the right and where the road curves to the right carry on straight ahead through a gate. At the house veer LEFT on the track to a gate. Go through and ahead along a waymarked track between two houses. Stay on this green lane until it ends at an old barn. Pass to the left of the barn over a stile. Carry on up the field (parallel to the long side wall of the barn) and through a gap in the wall ahead. Turn LEFT and through another wall gap. Carry on ahead, close to the wall on the left, to go over the most substantial historic wall crossing in the area. **Ignore** the wall gap now on the left and carry on ahead alongside the wall on the left. Pass to the left of the house which soon appears ahead and reach a waymark at a gate on the right. Go through and cross a stile in the fence ahead. Go LEFT across the field to another stile in a fence.

3 Cross the stile and walk up some steps to another waymarked stile in the wall on the left. Go over, then partly LEFT over some exposed surface rock. Then aim to go across the field passing to the right of some piled field clearance stones and on to a slightly raised path to a swing gate in the wall ahead. Go through and ahead alongside a low wall on the left. Cross the waymarked stile at the next wall and go through a small gate in the wall up ahead. Go ahead with a high wall on the left, but soon go half-RIGHT up to another similar small gate in the next wall. Pass through and then half-RIGHT ahead, passing to the right of a small rocky mound and

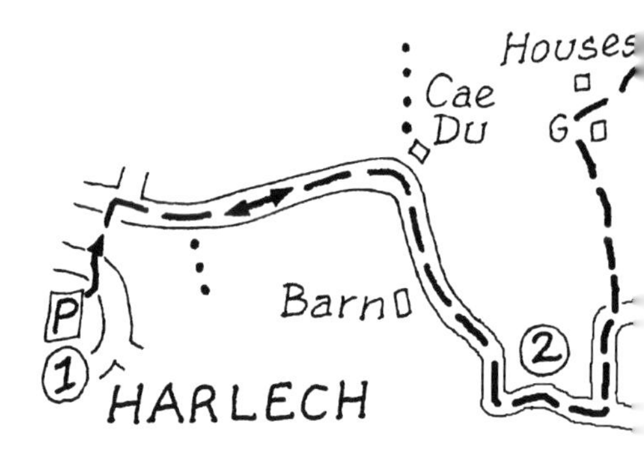

towards a group of isolated hawthorn trees. Go past and on ahead in the same direction towards the roof of the house Hendre-ddyfrgl which is now in sight. Keep on this line and pass left of the waymark ahead and down a faint track, still towards the house. When this track reaches another wider track at the wall below, go LEFT and then shortly RIGHT through a metal gate.

4 Go across the field and up through a small gate in the wall beyond Hendre. Keep ahead in the same direction and go through a metal gate in the next wall. Carry on through the next gate ahead and along the track to the farm Merthyr. Pass to the LEFT of the farmhouse and turn RIGHT immediately behind it, up along a rough surfaced wide track. This track leaves the farm area through a gate where a stone wall starts on the left. About 50 yards after this gate, and in an open area, go 90 degrees RIGHT, and pass to the right of a low rocky outcrop. At the crest of the field slope, aim for the gate ahead between a fence and a stone wall. Go through, carrying on slightly left, and reach a small metal gate in the wall ahead just to the right of the old stone step-stile crossing, which you may prefer to use. Do not go through the wide metal gate to the right in the same wall.

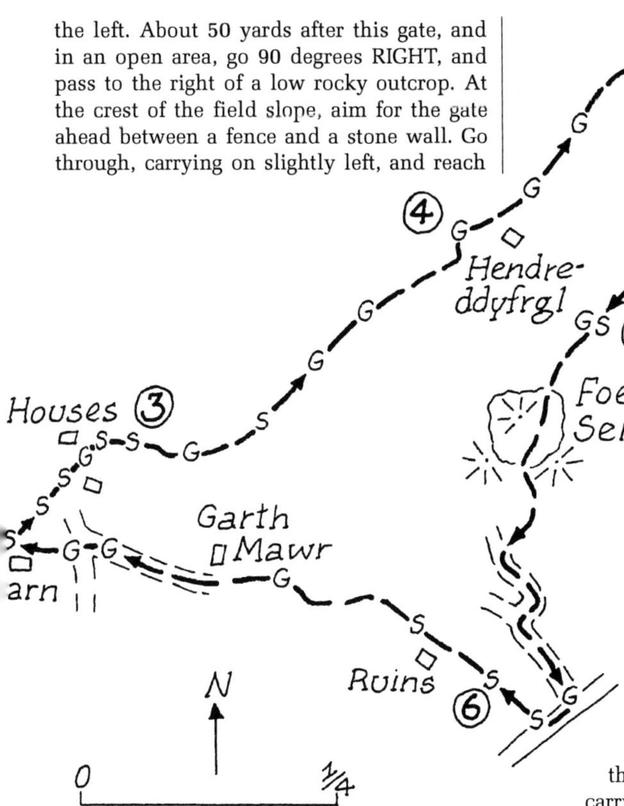

5 When through the wall, go LEFT uphill to the top. *Take advantage of the sturdy double-sided bench erected in 2002 in memory of Don Murphy who lived nearby and who loved the views here. At just over 1000 feet, Foel Senigl is the highest point on any of the six walks starting in Harlech and gives exceptional all around views. Snowdon to the north is 15 miles away, and the top of Bardsey Island, seen over the Lleyn Peninsula to the west, is twice that distance.* When you leave, carry on down the other side in roughly the same direction (southwards) finding the best way between the rock outcrops, and aiming for the high wall below. Near the wall, work RIGHT to reach a rough surfaced vehicle track. Turn LEFT along it and follow it down and out on to the road. Turn RIGHT along the road but in about 75 yards, go RIGHT over a stile and diagonally across the field, over a bridged small stream, and on through the gorse to a waymarked step-stile over the wall ahead.

6 Cross and carry on ahead approaching a stone wall with a fence on top. Do NOT go through the gate ahead but keep RIGHT, going along the wall and passing to the right of a ruined building. Just beyond the building, cross the wall through a small gated step-stile and carry on ahead. As another stone wall is approached, go LEFT and downhill. Follow close to the wall as it curves RIGHT, but when the wall curves right again keep on straight ahead towards an isolated large standing rock. About 20 yards before reaching this rock, go sharp LEFT towards the bushes and a wall. Find the stile over it at a waymark post, and cross. Continue up to the house Garth Mawr and cross the low wall to the left of the house. Turn RIGHT and go through the gate onto the vehicle track leading **up the slope** from the house. Continue along this track, later going through a gate. Shortly after this gate, and where another track joins it from the right, go RIGHT through a swing gate and down to the barn passed on the outward walk. Carry on along the lane to go between the houses, through the gate, and down the track to meet the road. Go ahead and at the T junction turn RIGHT to go back to Harlech.

WALK 4

MURIAU GWYDDELOD

(Irishmen's Walls)

DESCRIPTION This 2½ mile walk takes you up on the slopes behind Harlech for fine views, firstly over the beach to the Lleyn Peninsula and to the mountains of northern Snowdonia, and then later to the extensive range of the Rhinog mountains 5 miles east of Harlech. It passes an important ancient hut settlement (telephone 01766 780625 first if you wish to visit it).

START The Bron y Graig Uchaf long-stay car park (not to be confused with the Bron y Graig Isaf short-stay car park). See the map on the inside front cover.

1 From the car park go out on to the road and turn LEFT. Walk along to the end of the high stone wall on the right. Just beyond the gate where you can view the duck pond, take a narrow path off RIGHT alongside the first house. When it reaches a road, go RIGHT. *In about 100 yards there is a Scotch Baptist Chapel baptism pool created in 1841.* Carry on along the road, past the house Cae Du and up past an old barn on the right (*a listed building with graded slate roof and built, like many in this area, into the hillside slope often to give easy access at the back to an upper storage area*). Further along, the road turns sharp left. A few yards after this bend, go RIGHT, through a gate along a signed footpath. *From about here there are the first fine views back over the beach to Criccieth and the Lleyn Peninsula, the Glaslyn and Dwyryd estuaries, Portmeirion, and the high mountains of Snowdonia beyond.*

2 On reaching the farmhouse Cefnfilltir, follow the waymark direction LEFT towards the barns, then RIGHT through a waymarked gate and on ahead to go to the right of the barn facing you. Go through another gate, turn LEFT to reach another waymark and RIGHT through the gate as indicated. Keep ahead along the wide walled track until it ends in an open field. Go LEFT up alongside a wall, over a small stream and through a wide gap in an old wall slightly RIGHT ahead. Cross the same stream again ahead and go up through a gap in a substantial wall. At the open hillside take a route roughly diagonally across the field. As the crest of the hill top is being approached, aim for a large triangular shaped standing rock and, beyond it, a waymarked post. At the post, go LEFT to a fence-topped wall with a waymarked stile over it. *The extensive new views now ahead are to the east and the Rhinog mountains.* Cross the stile and the next one just 30 yards further ahead on to the road.

3 Turn RIGHT along it. After about 300 yards go over the signed ladder stile on the right. *In this field, just to the right (and marked on the 1:25,000 OS map) are two ancient hut groups known as Muriau Gwyddelod (or the Irishmen's Walls) with well-preserved foundations. They are interpreted as courtyard houses – circular huts within an enclosed yard, and called Enclosed Homesteads, thought to be occupied through pre-Roman and Roman times. They are part of much of pre-historic interest in this area of ancient landscape.* To continue the walk, aim diagonally (south-west) across the field in the general direction indicated by the sign at the ladder stile, to the western corner of the field where two walls meet. In the corner, cross the stone step-stile and go ahead alongside an old wall on the left. At the next corner go LEFT through a gap and then immediately very sharp back RIGHT to go along a walled grass lane ahead. After about 100 yards go through the gap on the right and then immediately LEFT along the wall to another gap ahead. From this gap go half-RIGHT across to a waymarked post and over a stone stile.

4 Go half-RIGHT across the next field, skirting to the right of a depression, and aim for a gap in the low wall ahead. Pass through and half-LEFT down to a low post waymark and on to reach a waymarked gate in the bottom corner. Go through and RIGHT

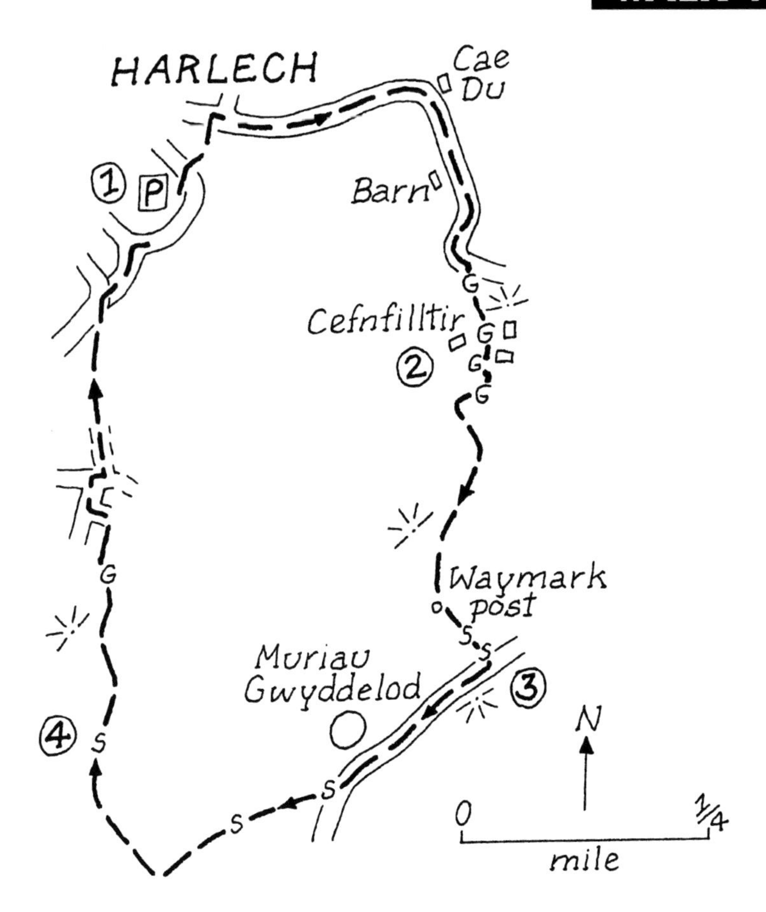

along a grass track to reach a road. Go ahead and RIGHT around three sides of a high wall. At the end of the final side, as a field gate is approached, go LEFT down a rough surfaced track past a domestic garage on the left, and into a shady lane. When this lane reaches a road go RIGHT. Where, very shortly, the road bends left for vehicles, keep on ahead and down to reach the car park.

About the author, Geoff Elliott

Geoff had strong feelings for the landscape of the old county of Meirionnydd. Always a very keen walker, he had known the area for 50 years. Born in Cardiff, and spending his working life there, he moved on early retirement to Dolgellau (where he wrote his other book in this series – **Local Walks Around Dolgellau**) and later to Harlech. He considered the area of these walks to be special, and wrote this book to help others discover and enjoy the attractions it holds. He was an active member of the Ramblers' Association and a voluntary Snowdonia National Park warden. Geoff died prematurely early in 2005, and is sadly missed.

WALK 5

HISTORIC STILES

DESCRIPTION A 4 mile walk into an area of quiet and beautiful countryside which few visitors see. On the way, and back, there are superb views and a chance to use interesting stiles left from another era.

START The Bron y Graig Uchaf long-stay car park (not to be confused with the Bron y Graig Isaf short-stay car park). See the map on the inside front cover.

1 From the car park go out onto the road. Turn LEFT, and in 20 yards take the track RIGHT up steps into a local nature reserve. *This area was originally part of the estate of a now demolished large house, Bron y Graig, and was acquired by the local authority in 1972.* Follow this path around to the right. After about ¼ mile it bends right and drops down. At the bottom take the narrow path LEFT. This path emerges at a rough surfaced lane. Go LEFT, then almost immediately RIGHT, following the high wall on your left. At the surfaced road go LEFT, keeping to the wall, and shortly LEFT again to reach a waymarked post. Go RIGHT, as indicated, along a grassy track to reach three gates. Go through the first gate immediately on the left and uphill with a wall on the right. Pass through the gap in the wall ahead and carry on uphill. Head for a large pile of field clearance stones and cross a stone step-stile in the wall just beyond it. Aim slightly RIGHT, and carry on uphill. *There are fine views back across the bay.* Near the top, go through a gap in the wall and then aim slightly LEFT for a waymarked post on the horizon. At the post carry on slightly RIGHT to another post on top of the stone wall ahead. Go over the stile and ahead to the next one. *There are now extensive views ahead to the rounded hill, Moelfre, and behind it and to the left, the mountains of the Rhinog range.*

2 Cross the road and go over the stile opposite. Take a route roughly half-LEFT. Head for the end of a stone wall and reach, in about 150 yards, a faint farm vehicle track. Turn RIGHT along it through a gap towards a barn. When at the barn, follow the track LEFT through a gate, keep on it through gaps in two low walls and reach a wall crossing the track. Stay on the track as it curves to the right alongside the wall. *There are now more extensive views ahead to the Rhinog mountains and to the coast well beyond Barmouth.* At the field corner keep on the track, now walled on both sides, to reach some barns. Pass to the right of the barns, through a gate and on ahead as waymarked. On approaching a line of trees ahead, curve around LEFT and through another gate. Follow the track down and curving right, and then out through a gate to the farm Tyddyn-du and a road. Go RIGHT, along the road for about ¼ mile to reach a double footpath sign.

3 Turn RIGHT here along the path up and over the rising ground then down, curving right, past high gorse and some oak trees, to reach laid stepping stones ahead approaching a wall. Go over the step-stile and carry on ahead uphill through the gorse. Go through a gate and continue uphill but near the top veer LEFT to a wall and a waymarked post. Go through and RIGHT, as indicated, up to another waymark on the right, then sharp LEFT along a wall. Continue LEFT to go past the house and to a rough surfaced vehicle track. After about ¼ mile, near the top of a rise, a metal gate is reached. Go through the **metal** gate and along the track to reach a surfaced road. Go RIGHT over the cattle grid and along to reach another cattle grid at a road junction.

4 Turn RIGHT here and go ½ mile along this road. 100 yards after the road enters a long straight stretch (*with fine views again east to the Rhinogs*) go LEFT at a double-signed stile (recognise it?) and then over the one in the wall 30 yards ahead. Continue ahead to the waymarked post. At it, go half-LEFT down and through a gap in the wall, then half-RIGHT down to the corner of the field.

5 **Care is needed as the walls are approached as there are two stone step-stiles over them.** Go over the one to the right.

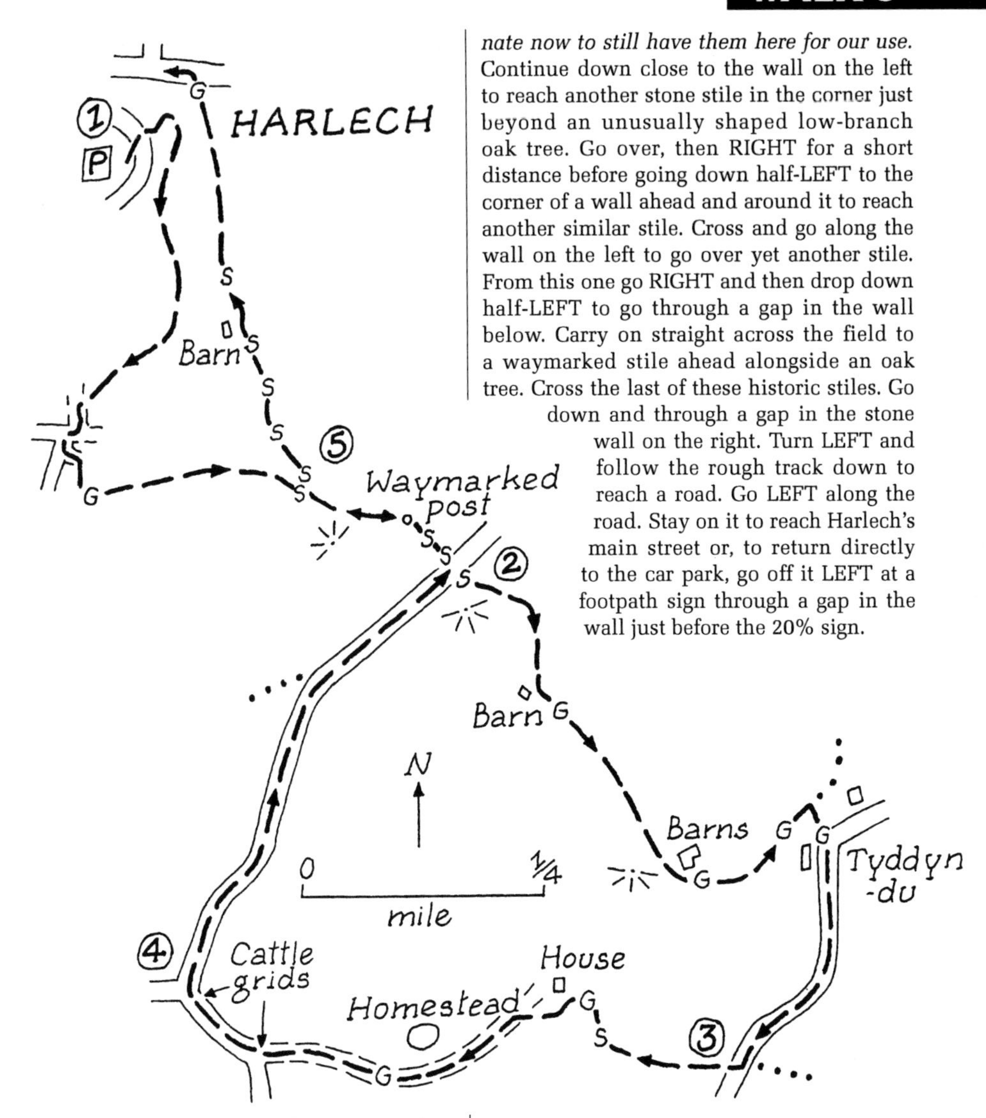

nate now to still have them here for our use. Continue down close to the wall on the left to reach another stone stile in the corner just beyond an unusually shaped low-branch oak tree. Go over, then RIGHT for a short distance before going down half-LEFT to the corner of a wall ahead and around it to reach another similar stile. Cross and go along the wall on the left to go over yet another stile. From this one go RIGHT and then drop down half-LEFT to go through a gap in the wall below. Carry on straight across the field to a waymarked stile ahead alongside an oak tree. Cross the last of these historic stiles. Go down and through a gap in the stone wall on the right. Turn LEFT and follow the rough track down to reach a road. Go LEFT along the road. Stay on it to reach Harlech's main street or, to return directly to the car park, go off it LEFT at a footpath sign through a gap in the wall just before the 20% sign.

This is the start of a number of these historic stiles, close together and constructed so carefully and substantially into the field walls. They were probably built about 200 years ago and this must have been a well-used route. To the chapels perhaps, to school, or to the market with baskets of local produce? Clearly not a serious commercial route as carts would have needed wall gaps. And when was it last used for its intended purpose? Whenever that was, we are fortu-

WALK 6

HARLECH BEACH via LLANFAIR CLIFF

DESCRIPTION This 4 mile walk, including just over 1 mile along the beach, first goes across the open countryside behind Harlech giving outstanding views over Tremadog Bay. It then goes through part of Harlech's quiet neighbouring village Llanfair, and to the top of high cliffs for the unexpected and stunning view of the whole length of the beach. The route then follows the fine zig-zag path directly down.

START The Bron y Graig Uchaf long-stay car park (not to be confused with the Bron y Graig Isaf short-stay car park). See the map on the inside front cover.

1 From the car park go out onto the road. Turn RIGHT along it and at the first T-junction go LEFT uphill. Where that road meets another coming up from the right, go LEFT along the road for 50 yards and take the signed path half-LEFT. When it meets a rough surfaced track at a high wall go RIGHT as waymarked. At the surfaced road go LEFT keeping to the wall, and in 30 yards, LEFT again to a waymarked post. Go RIGHT, as indicated, along the grass track. When three gates are reached, go through the recessed middle one and on half-RIGHT up the field to reach a low waymark post. Carry on as indicated, and through a gap in a low wall. Continue ahead, going very slightly LEFT, still rising and just skirting to the left of a natural depression. *It is worth pausing about here to look right and back for the extensive views. The Moelwyns on the extreme right (north), Snowdon (15 miles away) a little to the left and then the whole sweep of the Lleyn Peninsula with the top of Bardsey Island (30 miles away) just visible over the last section of land.* Keep ahead in the same direction and go over a waymarked stile in the wall.

2 Continue half-RIGHT up to another wall and the field corner. Go LEFT through the gap and follow the wall on the right. At the next field corner go RIGHT, through the gap and then LEFT along the green lane. When this lane ends at an open field, turn RIGHT and follow the stone wall. Keep straight ahead where the wall has a kink to the right, and ignore the wall gap. Continue on down to a stone stile. Do NOT cross it but go LEFT along the wall. At the end go out through a small gate onto the road and go RIGHT. Where the road bends right, go LEFT over the cattle grid and in 10 yards take the grass track half-RIGHT. When this reaches a metal gate, go through and half-RIGHT diagonally across the field, passing to the right of two large piles of field clearance stones. Near the field corner look for and go over the stone step-stile a little to the right. Carry on down ahead along the wall on the left. At this next field corner go through the gate ahead and carry on straight down to reach a green lane and go out on to a road. Turn RIGHT and reach a crossroads. *The chapel at this corner, Gaer Salem, was built in 1863.*

3 Cross and continue down to another cross roads. Go RIGHT and continue along the pavement for just over 100 yards until at the entrance to the property Murmur-y-Don and directly opposite the signed entrance to the National Trust property Allt y Mor. Cross the road with care and go through a gate. *It is then certainly worth using the nearby seat to enjoy the best possible view of Harlech beach: almost 4 miles of unspoilt dune-backed coast and with the mountains of northern Snowdonia far beyond.* When ready, go down the zig-zag path to cross the railway (TAKE GREAT CARE) and onto the beach. Go along it to the RIGHT (north) to reach the main exit at a wide gap in a fence safeguarding the dunes and where there is a high red and white pole. This sandy track soon becomes surfaced and joins a metalled road.

4 Continue straight ahead towards the Castle. At the end of this road turn RIGHT, and go through the gate on the right and follow the path to the left. After about

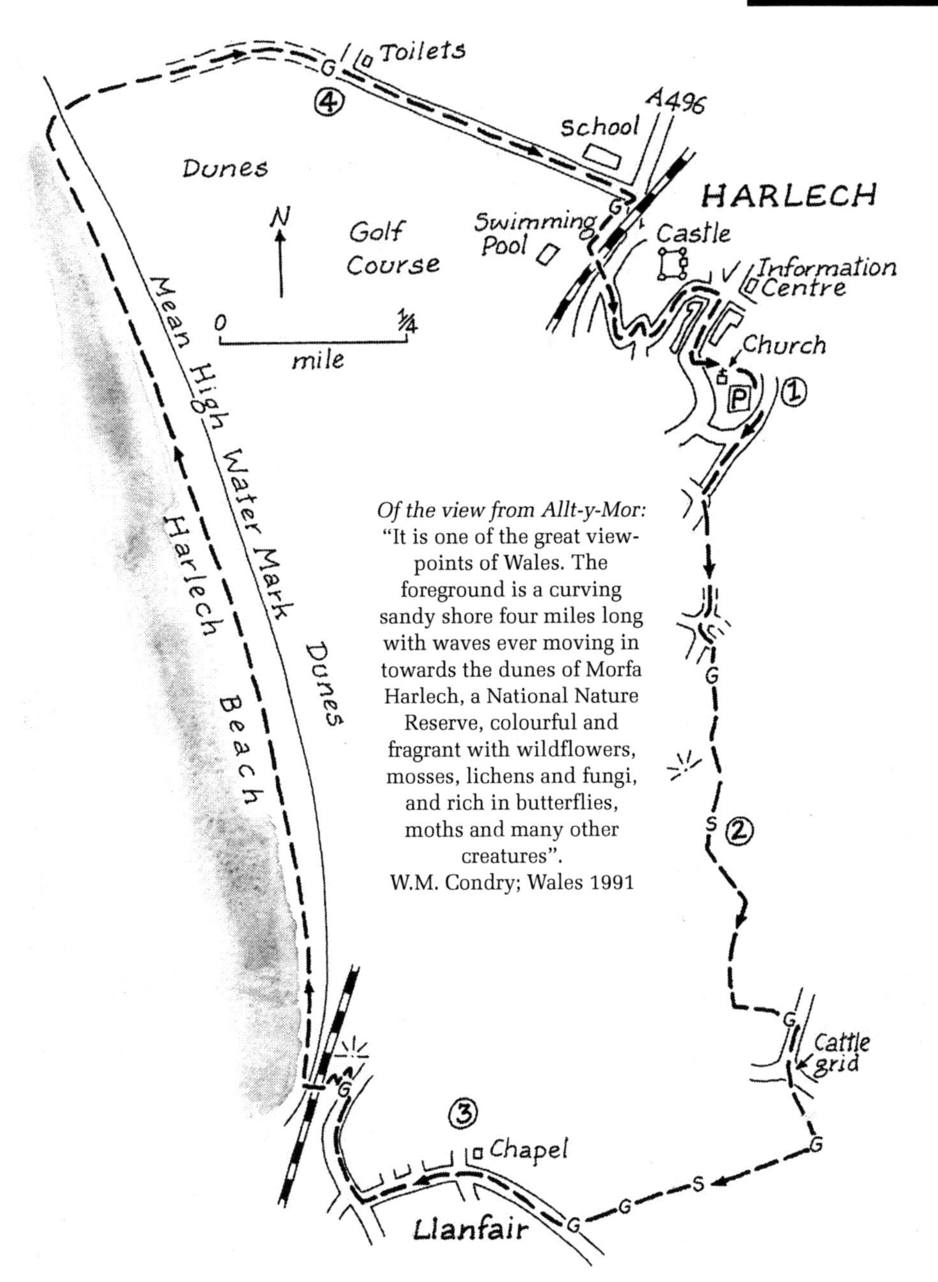

200 yards, where it is joined on the right by a path from the swimming pool, go LEFT to cross the railway and the main road. Go up the minor road signed 'Town Centre'. This zig-zags uphill (*there are seats!*) and where the road divides, go LEFT, past the 20% sign. When Harlech's main street is reached go RIGHT. There is a pleasant path to the car park off to the LEFT just before the Church.

WALK 7

YNYS

DESCRIPTION An easy 3½ mile walk giving a chance to experience an area very different from those in the other walks. There are pleasant fields from which there are fine views, an interesting church yard and a section along an estuary, part of a National Nature Reserve, where you will want to take plenty of time. Take binoculars, if you can, for the estuary birdlife. Care needs to be taken about the tide. The ½ mile section along the estuary would occasionally not be possible at some high tides, and **do not** attempt it if high tide is approaching. A board, usually on the road at the side of the old warehouse at Ynys, gives the high tide time.

START At Glan-y-wern, using a layby just beyond the hamlet, along the east side of the A496 at GR 606349.

DIRECTIONS Go north from Harlech along the B4573 (or the A496 if more convenient). After nearly 4 miles, at the junction of the 'A' and 'B' roads at Glan-y-wern, park in the layby just beyond (north) of the road junction (NOT, please, the layby with the telephone box in front of the houses).

1 From the layby, cross the road and go LEFT along it to the junction corner. Cross the river bridge and go over the second ladder stile on your right , and along the embankment top path, with the river – the Afon y Glyn – on your right. Carry on to cross the railway (TAKE GREAT CARE) using two stiles and continue ahead. *Portmeirion on the opposite side of the Dwyryd Estuary is now in view.* Cross two more stiles and continue, approaching the hamlet of Ynys. Go through a gate into the road and turn RIGHT along it. *The tall building (Ty Gwyn Mawr) was originally a warehouse. Ynys acted as the port for Harlech. Small ships would reach it, likely to be delivering coal and lime (there was a lime kiln at Llechollwyn). This area was also one of the various places along the estuary where boats were built, and was the landing for the ferry crossing from Porthmadog which, of course, discontinued soon after the railway and road bridge opened at Pont Briwett in 1867. There is a choice of seats at two locations when you reach the estuary. Firstly, at the end of this first straight section of road, second, a short distance further along the road on the rocks where the road ends at the next property Llechollwyn. Whichever your choice, it is certainly worth stopping to enjoy the birds and the views. Portmeirion is opposite. Far left, two miles away, at sea level across the estuary is Borth-y-Gest. To the right, looking up the estuary the mountains are the Moelwyns, and further right, some of the foothills of the Rhinog range and just a glimpse of the tops of some of the Rhinog mountains in the far background. A memorial plaque on one of the seats describes this as a special place, and who could disagree.*

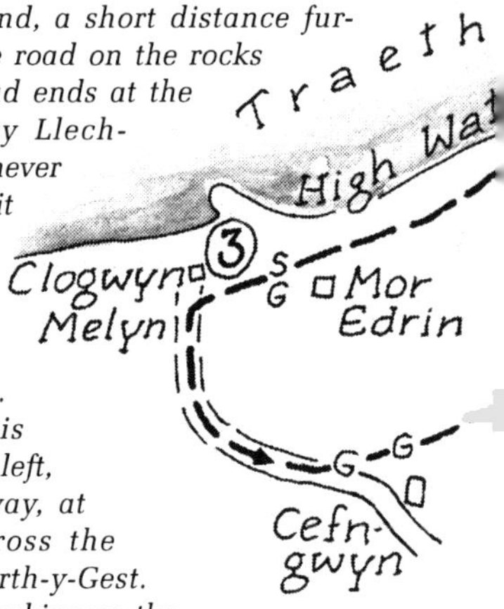

2 If you have not yet done so, continue along the road to its end at Llechollwyn. Continue ahead in the same direction, but now walking on the estuary grass. Your precise route can be determined by the state of the tide, and it can be interesting weaving between the small pools. The driest route is to keep up left, close to the exposed dipping rock and the line of trees above it. Whatever your route, eventually get to a large house (Mor Edrin) about ½ mile along the estuary, sited just up from the marsh area. At this house, go to a low stone wall at the edge of the marshland and walk RIGHT along it to a ladder stile in the trees near a gate.

3 Cross the stile and go ahead to a rough surfaced track at the property Clogwynmelyn. Go LEFT along the track for about ¼ mile to Cefn-gwyn Farm. Go through the road gate and then leave the road to go half-LEFT up to another gate in a fence. Go through and half-RIGHT across the field to a wall and fence. Bear LEFT along it to the corner where

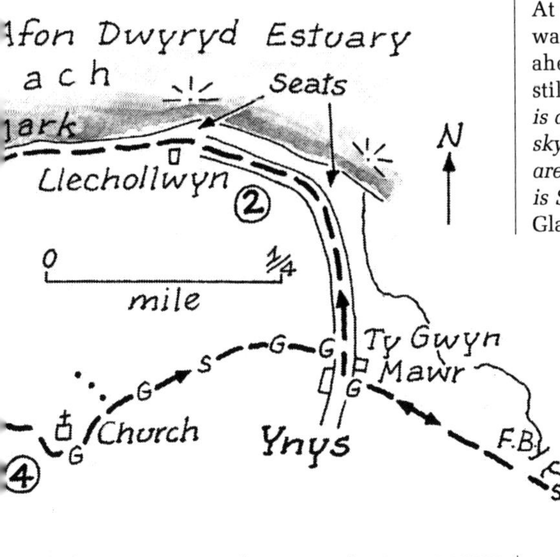

At the road go RIGHT, then just past the old warehouse, LEFT through a gate. Continue ahead **on top** of the 'sea wall'. Cross two stiles, then the railway. *Along this path there is a view to the right of Harlech Castle on the skyline, while up ahead is Moel Goedog, the area for Walk* **10**. *The lower hill further right is Senigl (Walk* **3**). At the road, turn LEFT for Glan-y-wern.

there is a covered water tank. Turn RIGHT and follow along the wall to the next wall corner. Here keep ahead in the same direction, along a faint path for nearly 50 yards to where there are then gorse bushes on your right. Go RIGHT along a narrow track through a gap in the gorse and keep along this path down to reach a gate in the fence below. Pass through the gate, down steps and up the other side to reach the church wall.

4 Go RIGHT along it to the church entrance. *This is 'St. Michael's on the shores' at Llanfihangel-y-traethau, probably on an island when first built, but becoming permanently linked to the mainland when the embankment between Glan-y-wern (where you started), and the Ynys warehouse was built in 1805. There is a note about the church at the door, and an interesting 12th century pillar gravestone closeby.* On leaving the churchyard turn LEFT and go through the signed gate. Follow around the church wall to a wall and fence. Turn RIGHT and walk with it on your left. Go through the gate **at the end** of the field and continue ahead to the next corner. Cross this interesting triple stone stile, and keep on in the same direction, but now with a fence close on your right. At the end of this field, go through a gate to a walled track and down to the road.

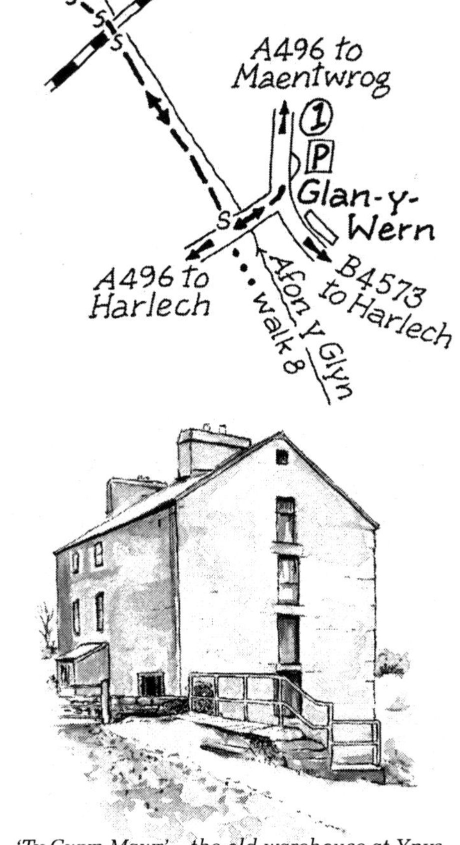

'Ty Gwyn Mawr' – the old warehouse at Ynys

WALK 8

AFON Y GLYN

DESCRIPTION A moderate 4 mile walk mainly along the deep narrow valley of the Afon y Glyn, the quietest and least well known of the river valleys near Harlech.

START At Glan-y-wern, using a layby just beyond the hamlet, along the east side of the A496, at SH 606349.

DIRECTIONS Go north from Harlech along the B4573 (or the A496 if more convenient). After nearly 4 miles, at the junction of the 'A' and 'B' roads at Glan-y-wern, park in the layby just beyond (north) of the road junction (NOT, please, the layby with the telephone box in front of the houses).

1 For safety reasons, from the layby go back (south) towards Harlech and the Glan-y-wern houses. When just past the road junction cross over the 'B' road, go back to the junction and turn LEFT to cross the river (the Afon y Glyn), and take the signed riverside footpath LEFT. Pass soon through two gates and continue on to reach the road. Go LEFT over the bridge and then RIGHT, along a minor road to reach, in about 200 yards, the cottage, Gefail y Cwm, on your left. Take the signed path through the gate, passing alongside the cottage and on through another gate and up a wide path ahead. *You are now in the quiet valley of the Afon y Glyn, where it runs for about 2 miles in a straight north-east/south-west direction. It is the least frequented of the valleys of the four rivers which start along the Rhinog mountains range and drain westwards to the coast, each of which has a markedly different character and which can be discovered by the walks in this book.* At the top of the rise keep straight ahead, as waymarked, into the trees. After about 100 yards, where the wide track divides, go half-LEFT downhill, staying on the broad track. The track passes an open field on the right and divides again as it enters woodland. Keep ahead RIGHT, walking slightly uphill and carrying on until a road is reached.

2 Cross the stile into the road, go LEFT, along the road and cross the bridge, Pont Dolorgan, over the Afon y Glyn. Stay on the road for about 250 yards and at a footpath sign on the right turn RIGHT through the Glanrafron gate. Stop to read the Tir Gofal sign on the left and Permissive Tir Gofal Map on the right. *Tir Gofal means 'land care' and is an agri-environment scheme in Wales. It supports farmers for protecting the archaeological heritage on their land, encouraging biodiversity, and for providing public paths.*

3 Go half-LEFT towards the trees. There is a Tir Goral waymark on the right. Go ahead to a gate. Go through the gate and continue along the river path until it climbs and you see a bridge on the right. *Notice the abundance of hard ferns (blechnum spicant) along the path.* Make a sharp hairpin turn LEFT and follow the path with the river on your left to a gate. Go through and up to a path. Turn sharp RIGHT along that path. Cross a stream and head towards two gates. Go through the gate on the RIGHT and stay on that path through heather and young oak trees. When two low stone walls meet in front of you at a right angle stay RIGHT with a low wall on your left and a slope with mature oak trees and giant royal ferns *(osmunda regalis)* on your right. At the end of a low wall on the left go AHEAD towards another wall on the left and a ladder stile. Go over that stile and ahead to cross another stile ahead. At the road turn LEFT and follow it around the lake, Llyn Tecwyn Isaf. Stay on that road, ignoring two surfaced roads that join it from the right. At a wide lay-by on the right leave the road and enter, by stairs, the Coed Cadw Woodland Trust forest, Coed Garth-byr. Follow that path until it takes you steeply back down the road.

4 Turn RIGHT along the road and RIGHT again onto the road which soon joins it from the right. Continue on this road up to the hamlet Soar. (Just before the first house there is a footpath sign on the left, and stone stairs. This footpath would take you down and across the river to the point where you entered the road at **2**.) About 100 yards past the last house on the left, go LEFT over the stile and ahead along the path. It soon bears slightly RIGHT to the top of a mound and ahead along the top. At the end, drop down towards a wall and gate. **Ignore and pass** the gate, and carry on with the wall on your left. Keep along this wall and go over the stile at the end. Go half-LEFT ahead. When a wall is seen on the left carry on ahead with the wall on your left. It eventually curves right and there is soon a gate. Go through, half-LEFT down and on ahead to trees and through a gap in a low wall. Keep on in the same general direction through trees with a wall over on the left. Go through the narrow gate reached and carry on down, keeping close to a wall on the right. When the track levels, and a field and road are seen over on the left, drop down LEFT into the field and curve RIGHT towards a gate onto the road. Turn LEFT along the road, over the bridge, and then RIGHT along the riverside path back to the start.

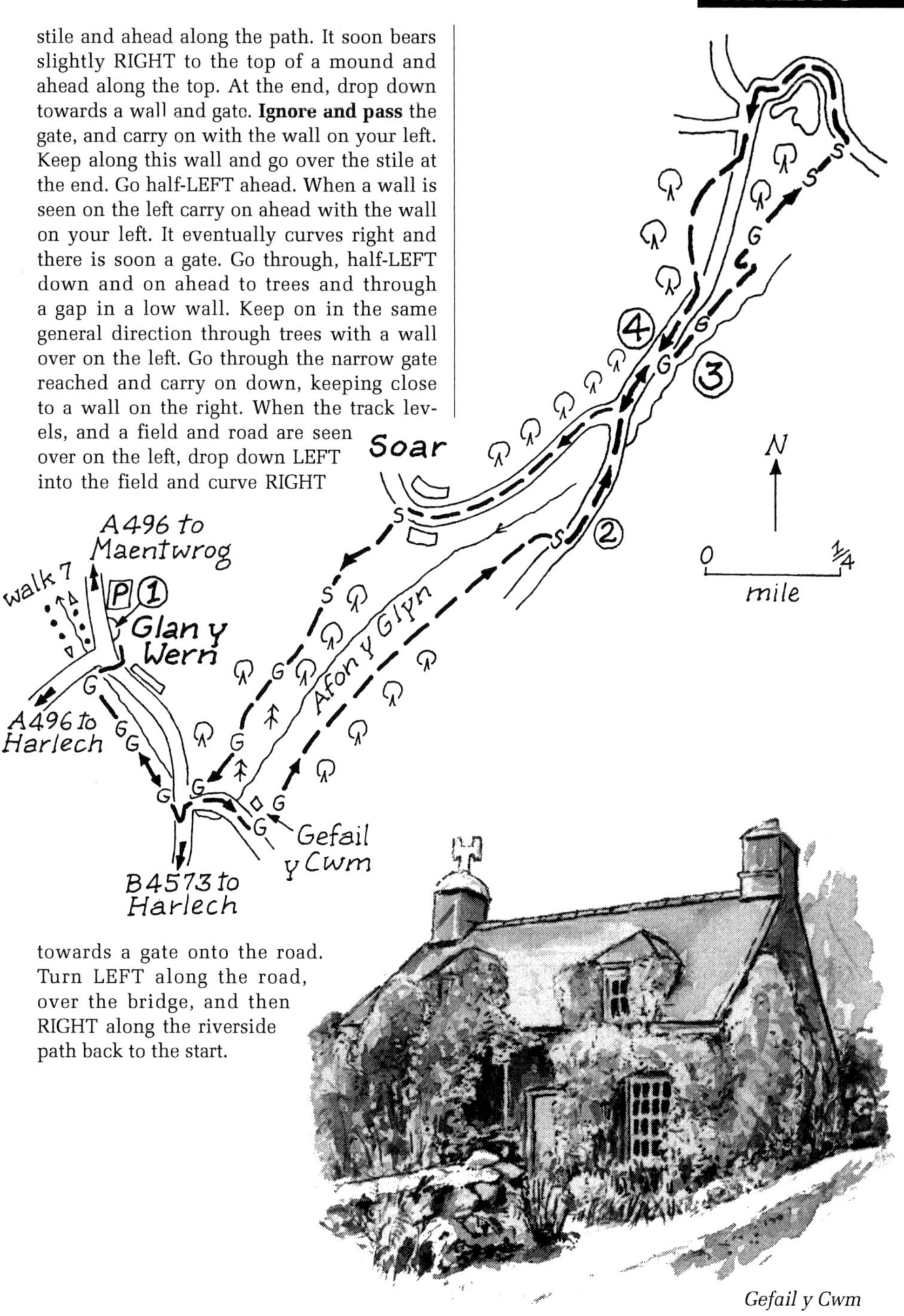

Gefail y Cwm

WALK 9

BRYN CADER FANER

DESCRIPTION A 6 mile moderate walk starting from a beautifully situated lake, continuing through woodland into an extensive open area of wild beauty, and to the site of a very distinctive Bronze Age stone circle. The central section of this walk, in open countryside, has few landmarks and the walk should not be undertaken in low cloud or mist. Parts can be boggy. Keep it for a fine day for the best rewards.

START Alongside the minor road at Llyn Tecwyn Isaf at SH 630371.

DIRECTIONS Go about 5 miles north from Harlech along either the 'A' or 'B' roads to Talsarnau. Just beyond the village turn sharp right along the road signed Soar and Llandecwyn. In **100 yards** take the partly concealed road left signed Llandecwyn. At a T-junction in just over a mile, turn left, then at the junction ¼ mile ahead, go right. Park alongside this road at the lake.

1 Carry on along the road going around to the east side of the lake. About ¼ mile after it leaves the lake go RIGHT at a road junction. In another 200 yards, where the road divides, go LEFT through the gate signed Caerwych. Continue up this road. *At the first sharp right turn uphill, Harlech Castle can be seen 5 miles away.* Go past Caerwych farmhouse and continue along the road through a wooded valley. *This road later opens out into extensive open moorland. The large rectangular stone building on the left was associated with a nearby copper mine.* Carry on along the road, past the interesting ruins of a fine barn on the right and on to reach the property, Nant Pasgan-bach.

2 Here go RIGHT at the signed track. Do NOT then go left through a wall gap but keep ahead, with the remaining section of wall on your left. Maintain this direction, aiming uphill towards the pass in the hills ahead, and soon getting close to a low wall on the right. You should now be on a faint wide track. Keep on it as it goes left around a large rocky outcrop and continues up towards the pass. Stay on this track. It bends left and goes towards the small ravine on the left. Further up the track divides. Keep LEFT on the main track across the now shallow ravine. It soon goes sharp RIGHT, up again towards the pass. Nearer the top the track again curves back left but soon sharply RIGHT. When the track eventually reaches its **highest point** and starts to descend, leave it and go RIGHT, directly to a ladder stile. *At the stile there are fine views back. The small lake, a mile away north, is Llyn Llenyrch; the mountains immediately behind it are the Moelwyns.*

3 **It is important now to follow these walk directions accurately.** Cross the stile and go partly RIGHT ahead towards a pointed rocky outcrop about 100 yards away. Pass close to the LEFT of this outcrop and continue on, same direction, up to the ridge ahead just left of a boggy reed area. Keep ahead on the same course, still keeping left of the large flat boggy area. When this reed area extends left across your route, go partly LEFT up to a large fin-shaped rock about 4 feet high. When you reach it, you will see that it is more than one rock. Just beyond these rocks, is a faint track which can be seen running to the right (south-west) and around the right side of a low mound. Go along this track. *The track is part of a prehistoric trackway thought to run from near Llanbedr on the coast to near Trawsfynydd. It is wonderfully rich in standing stones and evidence of ancient settlements, and it continued in use into Medieval times, being one of the important routes linking trading centres at Harlech and Bala.* After about 150 yards the track goes between two large mounds about 50 yards apart. The one on the right has much rock outcrop. Here the track divides, the one going left being a modern farm vehicle route. Take the track half-RIGHT, maybe losing sight of it going over boggy ground, but aim to **pass close to the end of the quartz-streaked, rocky mound on the right**. You will cross a narrow boggy stream. The track ahead then becomes more clear. About 200 yards after the quartz rocks there is a small length of high stone wall on the right, just 20

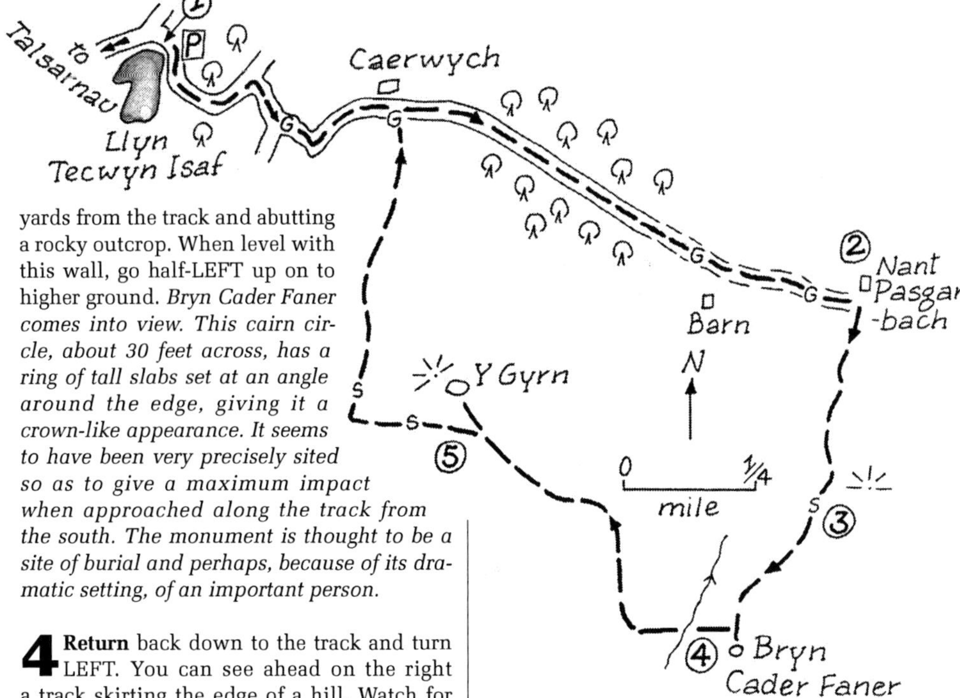

yards from the track and abutting a rocky outcrop. When level with this wall, go half-LEFT up on to higher ground. *Bryn Cader Faner comes into view. This cairn circle, about 30 feet across, has a ring of tall slabs set at an angle around the edge, giving it a crown-like appearance. It seems to have been very precisely sited so as to give a maximum impact when approached along the track from the south. The monument is thought to be a site of burial and perhaps, because of its dramatic setting, of an important person.*

4 **Return** back down to the track and turn LEFT. You can see ahead on the right a track skirting the edge of a hill. Watch for the junction with that track on the right. Turn RIGHT and work your way across a bog to follow the track. *Look for the remains of hut circles alongside the track on the right. Looking back from here, Bryn Cader Faner can be seen again.* In about 50 yards, the track divides. Keep RIGHT – it can be seen ahead where it is rock supported as it curves right. Stay along this track. When a large flat boggy area is reached the track itself becomes increasingly difficult to follow. It is best to keep on the right edge of this extensive flat area, close to the gorse covered slopes on the right. Continue around, but do not leave the flat area. *When at the far end of the flat area, just as Portmeirion and the estuary below come into view, and before your route starts to drop down, it is well worth going up the grassy slopes on your right to the top of Y Gyrn. At about 1000 feet there are superb views.* Leave the summit by the same route as you went up and rejoin the walk route. Continue along the base of the gorse slopes on your right. Below Y Gyrn, the track now goes steeply down.

5 At the bottom wall, go over the stile on the left. Go half-RIGHT ahead, down through a wall gap. Keep along the track down, and near the bottom go RIGHT, over to the low walls of an old rectangular structure 50 yards away. From here, go RIGHT to reach a ladder stile over a wall 75 yards away. Cross, and continue ahead with the wall on your left. In about 200 yards go LEFT through a wide gap in the wall (sometimes a gate). Go half-RIGHT along a track but **in just 25 yards** go LEFT, slightly down and along the edge of the reeds. This leads to a clear wide track. *Llyn Tecwyn Isaf soon appears down to the left ahead.* Keep along this track through two wall gaps (or gates?) to Caerwych Farm. Turn LEFT along the road and follow it back to the lake.

WALK 10

AROUND MOEL GOEDOG

DESCRIPTION An easy 5½ mile walk in open countryside with outstanding views, and along an easy-to-follow track. There is much of prehistoric interest.

START An open area alongside the minor road from Llanfair to Eisingrug, at SH 603316.

DIRECTIONS From Harlech go south to the Llanfair/Llandanwg crossroads on the A496. Turn left (east) and then left again at the next crossroads in ¼ mile. In another ¼ mile go right at the signed 'Cwm Bychan 6' junction. Stay on this road for about 3 miles to the entrance to Merthyr Farm, which is on the left about ¼ mile after crossing a cattle grid. Park (the landowner has kindly given permission) in the open area on the right. Please be careful not to block gates or hinder farm vehicles using the Merthyr Farm entrance.

1 Leave the parking area and continue north along the road. After nearly ½ mile, at a footpath sign, leave the road and take the track half-RIGHT. In about 100 yards the track divides. Take the LEFT fork and go through the gate 100 yards ahead. Carry on and through the next gate, and along the green track ahead. *The hill on your right is Moel Goedog, and at about 1200 feet, there are outstanding all round views from the top. If you wish to go up, there is a gap in the fence about 100 yards after the gate. At the top are the remains of an ancient hillfort, now divided by three stone walls. However, there are ladder stiles which allow those interested to examine the whole site.* **To continue the walk from the top** go over the stile on your left as you reach the top, and walk down that field to rejoin the track, and go RIGHT along it. **If you have stayed on the track**, in about another 50 yards after the fence gap, and just after the track starts to go slightly down, there is a Bronze Age burial ring cairn on the left. Continue along the track, through the next gate and on to go through another gate. *There are now superb views across the Dwyryd estuary and further north to the high mountains of the National Park. If the views make you want to stay longer in this area, it is possible to go to a secluded lake (Llyn y Fedw) by taking a faint track RIGHT just after going past a low wall about 300 yards after the last gate.*

2 The walk continues along the main track, eventually reaching a ladder stile in a wall ahead. Cross and carry on to the next wall and ladder stile in about 300 yards. Go ahead, with a wall down on your left but which later comes up close to the path. *Where it does, at a bend right in the path, a more remote and wilder peat-dominated area comes into view ahead with the mountains Ysgyfarnogod (just over 2000 feet) and, to the right, Clip, in the background. It is across this area that a Bronze Age trackway continues, and which is thought to have started near Llanbedr and taken the route of this walk so far. You may have noticed a number of standing stones along the road to the parking area, and afterwards, possibly to help indicate the easiest route in those times, along higher drier ground than the marshes below.* Continue now with the wall close on your left and reach a ladder stile with a low waymark post. The path over the stile continues along the ancient track, but for this walk follow the blue waymark ahead, keeping the wall on your left and best taking a faint path about 20 yards from it. After about 100 yards a tractor track (which has been in the tall grass close to the wall) is reached as it swings away from the wall. Go RIGHT along this track, up over the low ridge and down, curving right, to reach another blue waymark. Turn RIGHT as indicated along a similar green track and over a ladder stile at the next wall.

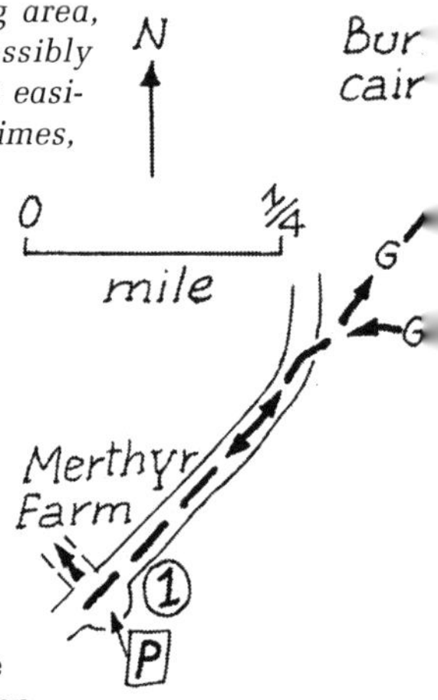

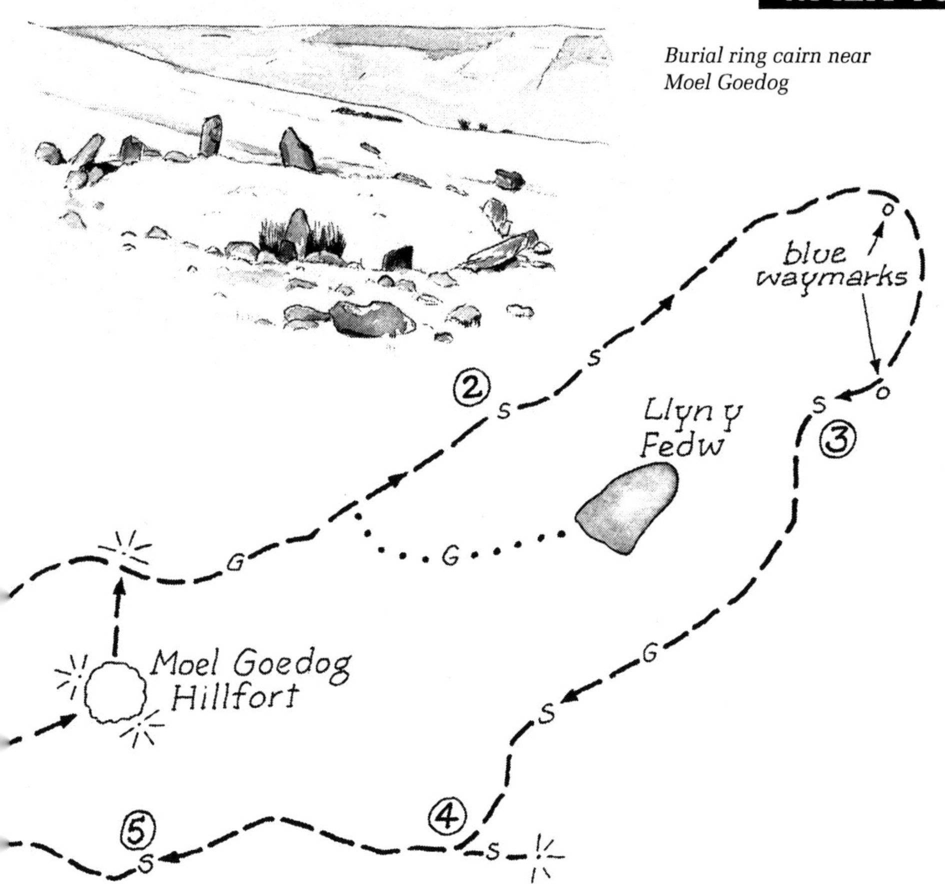

Burial ring cairn near Moel Goedog

3 Keep along this track, going through a gap in the next wall and now with a wall on your left. Reach a gate and go through along the track. It goes through a wall gap and on down to another ladder stile in sight ahead. Cross and continue along the track.

4 After about ¼ mile the track joins another close to a wall ahead, and where there are two ladder stiles nearby. One is ahead and slightly right, the other to the left alongside a gate. Go LEFT and over that stile, and walk to the top of the small mound ahead next to a wall on the right. *There are wonderful views into Cwm Bychan, with the lake visible. The high rounded mountain right of the lake is Rhinog Fawr (2362 feet), while over to the left are Clip and Ysgyfarnogod. You can even see Snowdon, well to the north.* Return over the ladder stile and continue along the clear track from it with a wall on your left. **Ignore** the stile over that wall and continue ahead to another ladder stile in about ½ mile.

5 Cross and go ahead along the track (rather faint). It soon curves left, and then right where there is a choice of tracks both going down to cross the lowest part of this area. It is best to take the track which is slightly left of the other. (**Note: the ladder stile way over on your left is not on your route.**) At the next wall ahead (the wall coming down from Moel Goedog on the right) the track curves left and goes through two gates and ahead to the road. Turn LEFT for the parking area.

WALK 11

LLANBEDR WOODLANDS

DESCRIPTION An easy 3½ mile beautiful low level walk. It will be appreciated especially by those who enjoy walking in superb natural woodlands.

START A little way along the minor road which leaves the A496 at the Victoria Inn, Llanbedr, at SH 585268

DIRECTIONS Go south from Harlech on the A496 to Llanbedr. In the village turn left (east) at the Victoria Inn, along the road signed Cwm Bychan and Cwm Nantcol. Park about 150 yards up that road on the left side just before the Ty Mawr Hotel.

1 Continue along the road (east) away from the village and turn LEFT at the next junction at the war memorial. Go past the houses and on beyond the last cottage, Tan-y-Wenallt. Ignore all footpath signs until, about ½ mile after Tan-y-Wenallt, the next house (Hen Bandy) on the right is reached. Just before this property go RIGHT at a waymerk sign up into the wood. After a gate, keep going up along the path slightly right, and after a stony section where a path joins from the right, go LEFT keeping along the main path. A surfaced drive at The Ranch, an outdoor discovery centre, is soon reached. Turn LEFT along it, through the car parking area, and out into an open field on the right. Stay on this drive until just before it bears sharply left. Here, go partly back and very sharply RIGHT diagonally across the open field. Near the top go over LEFT to a stone step-stile in the wall next to a fenced enclosure.

2 Go over the wall and follow the path to a wall with a gate and stile. Go through and continue half-LEFT, then RIGHT to the next stile visible just over 100 yards ahead. Cross and go straight ahead (**not left**) for 25 yards to the start of a wide path right. *Here, the narrow path straight ahead up on to the top of the rock outcrops, and then going slightly right, takes you to an ancient hut circle.* However, the walk continues along the wide path RIGHT, passing to the left of a fine oak tree and the back of a former cottage. Keep on down to an interesting metal stile. Cross and carry on ahead, and in about 50 yards, at a junction of walls, keep ahead between two walls to a gate. Go through and follow close to the wall curving LEFT to reach a farm. Pass to the RIGHT of the house and up to a rough surfaced track. Go LEFT along it, down, to cross a cattle grid at a barn. Turn RIGHT through the second gate and go ahead with a wall on your right. *A fine view from here, to the right, of Moelfre – the area of Walk* **15**. Go through the wall gap ahead and along the path half-LEFT. Keep to the right of the boggy area close to a fence on the right and head towards an old field wall. Go along the wall to a stepped gap and go through into the wood.

3 In 25 yards, at a main track, turn RIGHT. Keep along this beautiful woodland track for nearly ½ mile, and go through a small gate. Continue half-LEFT and in about 100 yards reach a waymark post on the left. At this post, a path junction, turn very sharp RIGHT and go down a path in this new direction soon passing old buildings to reach a gate. Go through and keep ahead, passing a waymark, to another gate. Go through to the gate ahead and on up to reach a wide rough surfaced track. Go LEFT along this track. Ignore the similar track right after about 100 yards, keeping ahead bearing slightly LEFT, and dropping down. *On this section there are fine views up Cwm Bychan.*

4 In another 200 yards, as you meet trees and a fence ahead, turn very sharply RIGHT along a similar rough track. Stay on this track going past farm buildings on the right, and passing the house Penrallt, and continuing ahead along a wide track close to a wall on your left. Go through a gate and continue along the wall. Stay with it when it curves left and drops down to a gate. Go through, down to the road, and go LEFT along it back to Llanbedr.

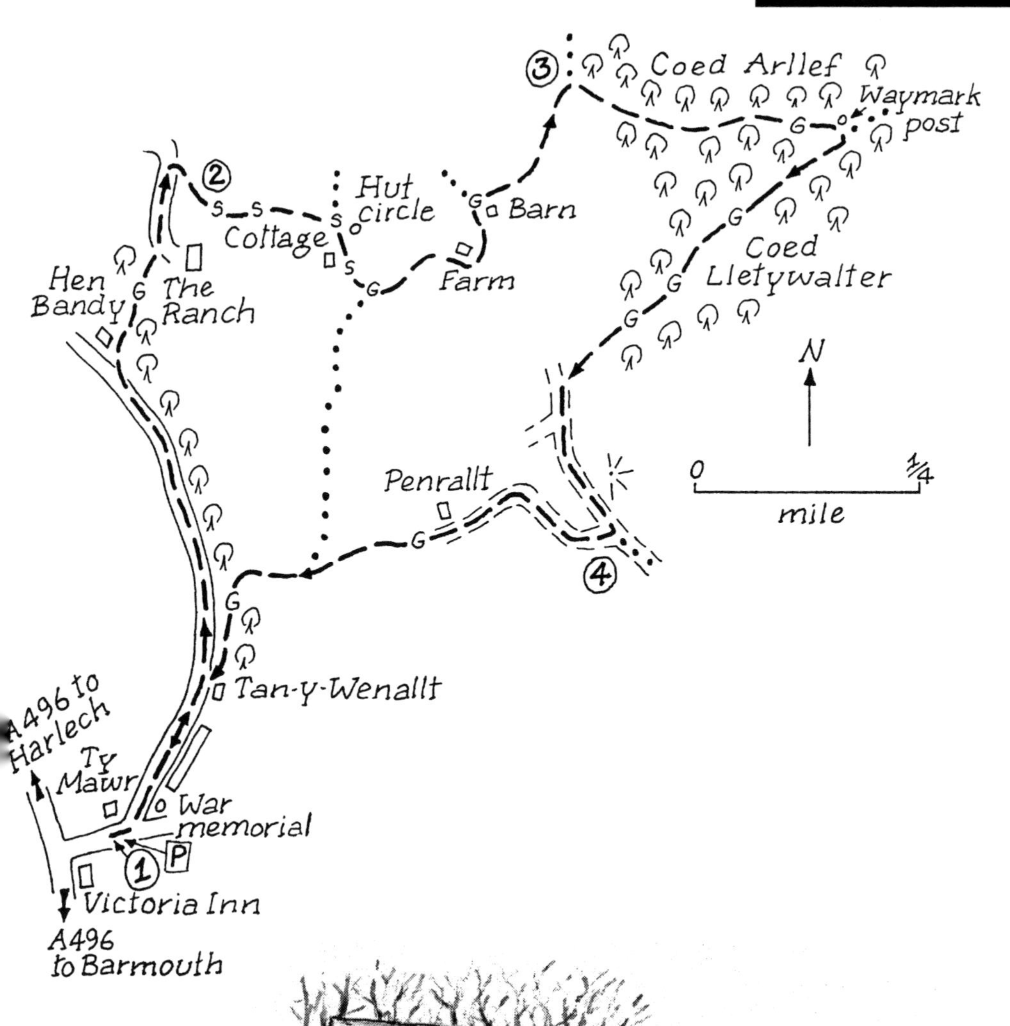

Capel Salem
(Walk 12)

WALK 12

CAPEL SALEM & THE AFON ARTRO VALLEY

DESCRIPTION A 4½ mile easy, low level, walk in mixed and very attractive countryside using some fine walled green lanes, and including a visit to a chapel featured in probably the most famous 'Welsh' painting.

START Along the start of the minor road serving Cwm Nantcol, at SH 601272.

DIRECTIONS Go south from Harlech on the A496 to Llanbedr. In the village turn left (east) at the Victoria Inn, along the road signed Cwm Bychan and Cwm Nantcol. In just over 1 mile, turn right (signed Cwm Nantcol) to cross the river, then first left. Cross the cattle grid and park on land alongside the river a little way up on the left.

1 Carry on up the road to Salem Chapel, with the Afon Artro on your left. *It is Salem Chapel in which Curnow Vosper painted, in 1908, the picture which has hung in thousands of Welsh homes, and was exhibited at the Royal Academy in 1909. The original, bought later that year by Lord Leverhulme, is in the gallery at Port Sunlight, but a copy is of course in the Chapel. Were it not for the popularity of the painting, Salem would probably not be a chapel of such interest. But it is a fine example of a Baptist chapel, with a plain unpretentious interior where the emphasis was on the 'word'. It was built in 1850. Before that, worshippers met in one of the row of cottages below, where you have parked, and it was the river (the Artro), just below Salem, which was used for baptisms.* After visiting, continue on past the Chapel. IGNORE the first footpath sign on the left in 30 yards, but at the second path sign in another 30 yards go LEFT. Go up into a walled track and curve left to reach a gate. Pass through and keep on ahead alongside a wall. At the wall corner carry straight on and through the wall gap directly ahead. Maintain the same direction, eventually reaching a swing gate at the top corner of this large field. Go through and ahead to pass to the left of the property Y Fron.

2 At the surfaced drive go LEFT along it down to the river bridge at Pen-y-bont. Go RIGHT along the road for 75 yards, then LEFT over the stone step-stile. Follow along the wall on your left to the way-marked stile ahead. Cross and go half-RIGHT to the farm barns. Go through the gate just beyond the first barn, go RIGHT and through another gate, and over a cattle grid to a road.

3 Go straight across and through a gate. At the end of the wall on your right, go half-RIGHT to reach a small river and the course of an old leat. *This leat served a tannery, the ruins of which are along to the right.* Bear LEFT and through a way-marked gate to follow a route alongside the wall on your left. Go through the gate at the end of the track and bear RIGHT, passing a barn on your left and on to another fine section of walled lane. At the junction ahead turn LEFT. Go through the gate at the end of this length and continue along the track half-RIGHT.

4 On reaching farm ruins (Blaidd Bwll) turn immediately LEFT after going through the gate, and go through a way-marked gap. Continue ahead along the ditch and line of trees on your right. In about 100 yards, where the ditch meets a wall coming from the field on the right, and where the ditch is bridged, go half-LEFT to a way-mark post. Go sharp LEFT as waymarked, and on to pass to the left of an isolated oak tree and over another bridged ditch. Keep ahead, through a wall gap and then half-RIGHT across to a wall corner. At this corner, do NOT turn left but go up ahead through gorse. The farm Tyddyn Rhyddid comes into view. Bear LEFT to reach a swing gate in the wall below. Go through and ahead, through two more gates close together, and continue ahead along the wall. When a fence is reached ahead, go LEFT along it and out through a gate to the farm drive. Go LEFT, through another gate, to the road.

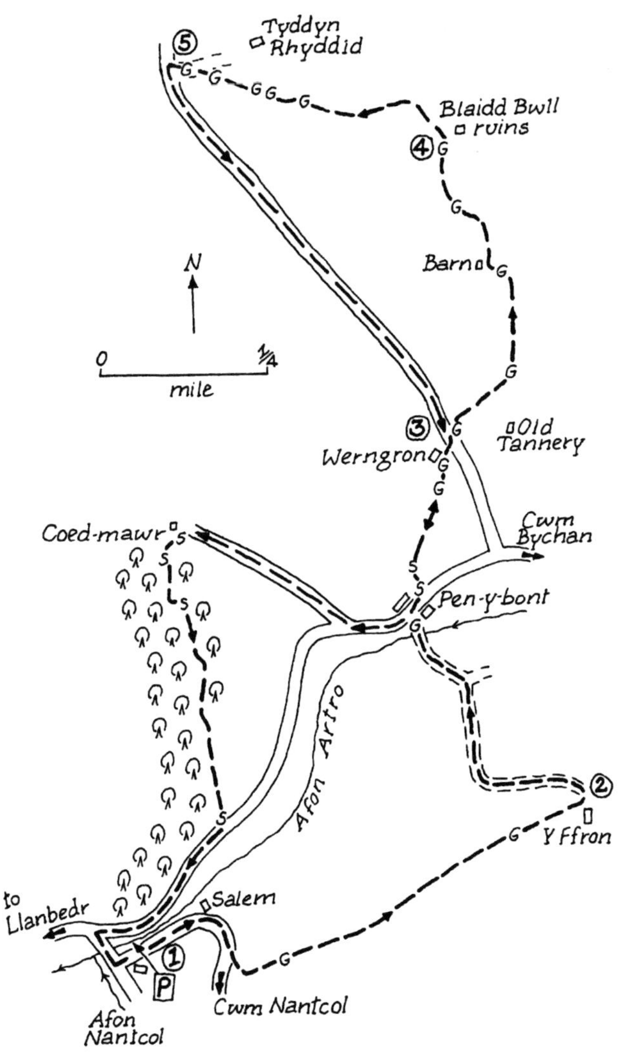

5 Turn LEFT at the road and walk along it back to Werngron. Retrace your route across those fields and stiles. Turn RIGHT and walk through Pen-y-bont. After a few hundred yards on the road turn RIGHT onto a track marked with a footpath sign. Stay LEFT on that track through a gate and follow the track to the house, Coed-mawr. Go through a gate into the house grounds. Turn LEFT into the wood over a stile. Follow along the wall on your left and where it later joins another wall and goes ahead, go LEFT through a wall gap. In a short distance go over the stile in the wall now on your right and continue ahead and down with a wall on your right. At the bottom turn RIGHT along a flat area parallel to a fence on your right. Keeping reasonably close to the fence, drop down a slope to trees below, curving to the right. Carry on, and where a wall appears ahead, bear LEFT and walk with this wall on your right. At a stone step-stile ahead, cross and go RIGHT along the road by the Afon Artro and back to the start.

WALK 13

CARREG FAWR

DESCRIPTION This fine walk is included for experienced hill-walkers who enjoy a challenge of route finding in open country. *It should **not** be undertaken in low cloud or mist.* Although only about 4 miles and with a straight forward start, it is not all an easy stroll. But it is very rewarding: the beautiful Artro river valley to start, then native woodland, followed at about the 1000 foot level by thick heather and moorland from where there are superb views. Reduction in sheep numbers has helped the heather growth, and it is spectacular when in bloom in August. But it means in some places that an actual path is difficult to find; bracken too can be challenging. In these circumstances our map can usefully be supplemented with the OS map Explorer OL18. There are four key points on the walk which it is essential to reach. They are shown **A**, **B**, **C** and **D** on the map in this book and their grid references are given in the walk directions.

START Park along the minor road from Llanbedr to Cwm Bychan at Pont Cwm-yr-afon, at SH 622298 (small charge).

DIRECTIONS Go south from Harlech on the A496 to Llanbedr. In the village turn left (east) at the Victoria Inn, along the road signed Cwm Bychan and Cwm Nantcol. At a road junction in just over 1 mile, keep straight ahead along the Cwm Bychan road. In about a further 2 miles park on the right **by the river bridge** (the second, not the first, of two similar riverside parking areas.)

1 Walk back down the valley road for about ½ mile to Crafnant Farm on your right. In a further 250 yards, go half-LEFT through a gate down to cross the river at Pont Crafnant. Follow the track RIGHT, passing left of an old barn and over a ladder stile. Keep along this track up through the wood. *On your right is the Coed Crafnant Nature Reserve owned by the North Wales Wildlife Trust and described as a fine example of ancient woodland rich in mosses, liverworts and ferns. Well worth a visit on another day.* When you reach an open area the track splits. Take the feinter grass path half-RIGHT uphill. DO NOT continue on the track ahead. Pass close to the left of an old stone building. Continue uphill in the same direction. When the first trees are reached at the top of the open area go RIGHT into the next open area and stay on that course. When the next trees are reached, keep ahead to reach a fence and wall. Go up LEFT along it to a small gate and ladder stile. (This is **A** on the map, at GR 623289, and the first of the four key location points.)

2 This is the end of the wooded area. Cross the stile and continue uphill, along the track from the gate, and leading roughly east. Stay along this track until it ends at a gap in a low wall. Continue up in the same general direction, sometimes alongside boggy areas and increasingly in heather and perhaps bracken. You will reach a low old wall on your right. DO NOT cross it but keep on the left of it to where it turns sharp left across your route. At this corner, go through and continue up in the same direction. Pass to the right of a heathery mound, and soon a high wall is in sight ahead on the right. Go up towards it, and bear LEFT to reach a wall gap in it. (This is **B** on the map at GR 627291.)

3 Go through the gap and find a way half-LEFT ahead to go along the right side of a very low line of rocks. A (probably hidden) path further ahead then zig-zags up the slope in front through thick heather. If you cannot find this 'path', make your way up as best you can, keeping the high wall on your left in view. In about 250 yards you will come to a ladder stile high up in the wall on your left. (This is **C** on the map at GR 629292, the third key point.)

4 Cross and go straight ahead through the heather. In about 50 yards, the narrow path bears right. At this point you can turn LEFT and work your way up to the top of Carreg Fawr through heather and over rock slabs. Go up to reach a stone cairn at the very top. *This is Carreg Fawr at about 1000 feet, and there are superb all-around views.* When you must leave, go back down near the lad-

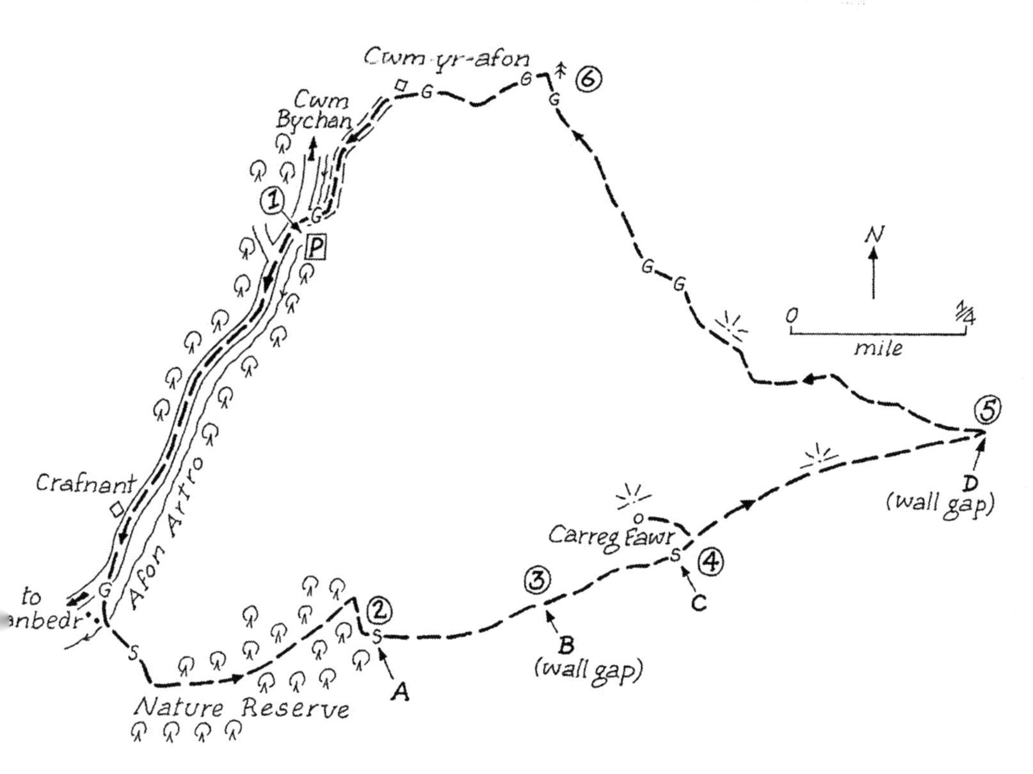

der stile. With the ladder stile at your back go half-RIGHT across the moorland. Some small tracks are visible, and you should be walking roughly parallel to a wall up on your right, and then gradually getting closer to it. When you reach the wall follow it. When the wall drops down you will see a grassy track below on the left which has come through a gap in the wall at GR 637294. Drop down a steep path to join that track. (This is key point **D** on the map.)

5 *This wall gap is where an old mineral track passes through to former workings up ahead.* DO NOT go through the gap, but go LEFT, westwards, along and down the track. Keep on this track for nearly a mile as it drops down to the valley bottom. *There are glorious views all the way.* Where the track levels out at a wall on the left go through the gate on the left. Turn RIGHT on the track and go through another gate. Continue down.

6 Go through the gate at the bottom and straight ahead to join another track just past the trees. Turn LEFT to the next gate and stay along the track ahead. Continue on through another gate, and pass to the left of Cwm-yr-afon Farm. Bear LEFT along the farm track back to the start.

WALK 14

CWM NANTCOL

DESCRIPTION A moderate 6 mile walk partly along the valley floor and partly up on the northern slopes. Wonderful views in open countryside. It is a walk which allows a fine appreciation of this beautiful valley.

START Along the minor road serving Cwm Nantcol from Llanbedr, at Capel Nantcol. SH 623262

DIRECTIONS Go south from Harlech on the A496 to Llanbedr. In the village turn left (east) at the Victoria Inn, along the road signed Cwm Bychan and Cwm Nantcol. In just over 1 mile, turn right (signed Cwm Nantcol) to cross the river, then first left. In a further 2 miles at Capel Nantcol (where there are a telephone box and a post box on the right) park in the space on the left.

1 From the parking area take the adjacent signed path through a gate down towards the river (north). Shortly, go through another gate and turn RIGHT along a wall. At the next gate in the wall and by a waymark post, go LEFT to reach a waymark post 100 yards ahead. **Because of the drainage ditches in the valley, often hidden from view, it is important to follow the walk directions very carefully, otherwise the small bridges across them may not be found.** Continue in the same northerly direction across the rough grass to another waymark post in about 150 yards where a drainage ditch is bridged. Keep again in the same direction ahead to a yellow topped post, at the river, and turn RIGHT to a footbridge.

2 Cross and walk ahead with a drainage ditch on your left. In 30 yards, curve LEFT aiming towards a small spur of rock outcrop jutting into the valley floor. Follow, on your left, another ditch, and go to the low waymark post just left of the rock spur. Here cross the slab bridge and go half-RIGHT. The Afon Cwmnantcol is on your left. Begin to look for the ruins of farm buildings and a wide metal farm gate on the slope just above the reedy area to your right. That is your destination. When the river makes its second sharp curve to the left look closely on your right for a low plank footbridge with low posts across the ditch. Turn RIGHT there and cross the bridge. There will be a ditch on your left. Go across the reedy area and up to the wide metal gate in front of the farm building ruins

3 Go through the gate, up to the left of the buildings, and on up an old track. Cross over the stile at a fence and go LEFT along a wide track. Keep along this track until, in nearly ½ mile, it joins a road. Go LEFT and carry on to the main valley road. Here, go RIGHT, and about 100 yards after the **second** house (Gelliwaen) turn RIGHT up a wide rough track, passing to the side of a gate, and continuing up for ¼ mile to another gate.

4 Go through, and then RIGHT along a wide grass track. *There are soon fine views over the valley. Keep a look out for wild goats.* The track curves left, and after a long straight stretch uphill it curves again slightly left. About 50 yards after this bend, at a path junction, take the **partially concealed** similar grass track half-RIGHT. After 300 yards, cross a stile and continue along the track. At the next wall go through the gate and ahead. Go through another gate in about 300 yards and continue with a wall on your left. Go over the ladder stile at the next wall and LEFT along the wall. **Ignore** the ladder stile and gate in the wall on your left after 250 yards, and continue on to reach a gate in a wall **across** your route. Go through and ahead along the track keeping along it as it later curves slightly to the right, away from the wall, and passing to the left of an area of large rocks. As the track approaches the last, rather isolated, higher rock outcrop, follow it RIGHT and on through a wall gap. Stay on the track up to a ladder stile and gate in a wall 300 yards ahead. *The trench up on the left is the line of former manganese workings, much evidence of which will be seen along this section of the walk.* Go over the stile and ahead along the lower (right) of the two tracks leading from the gate. When another ladder stile comes into view work LEFT to cross it. Keep ahead along this old mineral track. In 150 yards, you reach the ruins of

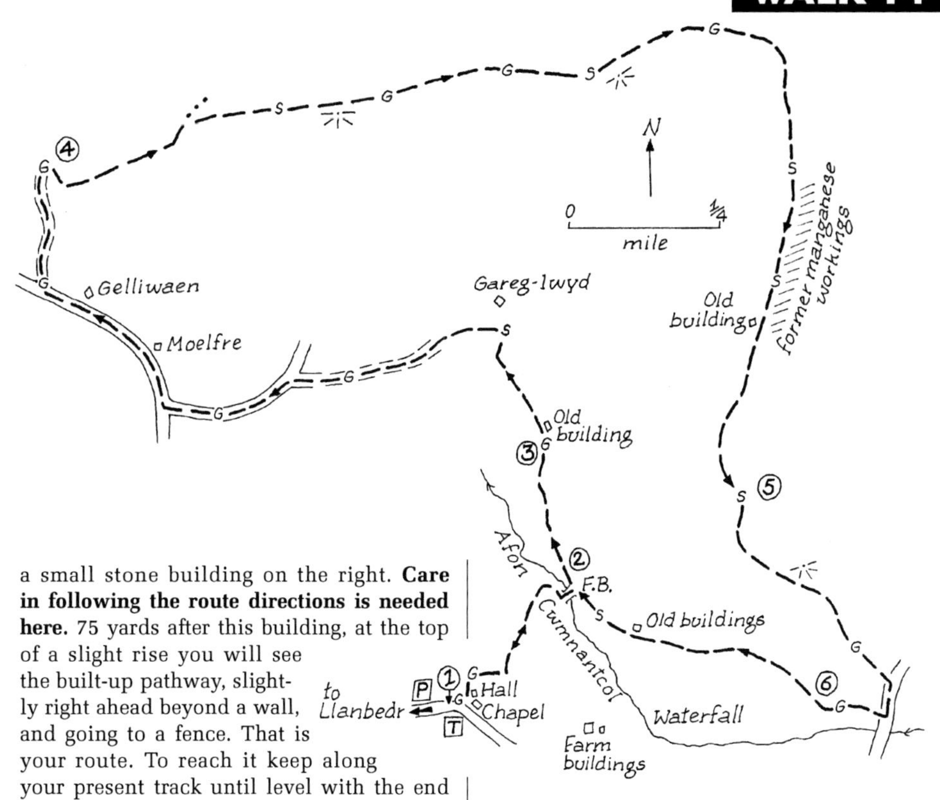

a small stone building on the right. **Care in following the route directions is needed here.** 75 yards after this building, at the top of a slight rise you will see the built-up pathway, slightly right ahead beyond a wall, and going to a fence. That is your route. To reach it keep along your present track until level with the end of a mineral working trench on the left. A few yards after this, **leave the track** and go half-RIGHT steeply down a faint narrow path between some rocks. Go steeply down past a mine entrance, on through the wall gap and ahead. Continue along the fence on your right (taking care with the barbed wire) to reach a ladder stile. Cross and go down ahead.

5 *Soon the grass topped Y Llethr, the highest of the Rhinog range at 2475 feet is directly ahead. Flat topped Rhinog Fach is to its left. Across the valley to the right is Moelfre, the core of Walk* **15**. Keep on down, through a narrow wall gap, ahead across sloping rock surfaces to a gate in a wall below on the left. Go through and along the path ahead, then RIGHT through a wall gap in 100 yards and half-LEFT to the road. Go RIGHT, and RIGHT again to the left of the footpath sign just **before** the road bridge. Cross the field to the gate 100 yards ahead.

6 Go through into this geologically very interesting area and half-LEFT across rock slabs. Follow the path as it curves right, through a small wall gap and on to a waymark post. Follow that arrow to a sloping rocky outcrop. Go over the tip of the outcrop and stay close to it to keep out of the boggy area on the left. Go to the next waymark now visible. Carry on as indicated using the four more waymarks placed at intervals of about 100 yards, eventually dropping down to the valley floor at a waymarked wall gap. Go half-RIGHT across to a yellow-top post and continue on, passing to the left of old buildings, to some trees. Here go half-RIGHT as indicated, to a ladder stile. Cross and go ahead half-RIGHT, soon with a drainage ditch on your left, to the footbridge. Cross and turn RIGHT. At the yellow-topped post ahead go LEFT to a waymark post and on to reach the wall ahead. Turn RIGHT to get back to the start.

WALK 15

AROUND MOELFRE

DESCRIPTION An easy 5½ mile walk around the base of the rounded 1900 foot hill, Moelfre, 5 miles south of Harlech, and which stands detached from the nearby Rhinog range of mountains. It is a walk in open country with outstanding views, providing a chance to sample the expansive wildness of the Ysgethin valley, and to give thought to the stagecoaches that crossed it in the 18th century.

START Along the minor road passing on the north side of Moelfre at SH 614258.

DIRECTIONS Go south from Harlech along the A496 for about 5 miles to Dyffryn Ardudwy. Before the village centre, and about ½ mile after passing the 30 mph signs, take the road left (east) signed 'Cwm Nantcol 3½'. At a skewed crossroads in 1½ miles, go right then immediately left (Cwm Nantcol). In another mile park on the left in an open area just past an old quarry on the right.

1 Walk back along the road (south-westerly) towards the sea. *In about ¼ mile, at a swing gate on your right, visit Ffynnon Enddwyn, an ancient well said to have curative properties. A board at the well tells you more.* After another ¼ mile, take the signed wide track LEFT up across open country. This leads to a corner where four walls meet. Go through the gate and small sheep pen and go RIGHT, parallel to a wall on the right. *The undulations up on your left are the results of manganese mining which ceased about 100 years ago.* Keep along the wall and go through a gate at the end of the field. Carry on in the same direction with the wall on the right and go through another gate. Continue ahead and reach a footpath sign at a wide track. Go LEFT along it and soon through a gate. *This is part of the old coach road from Bontddu to Llanbedr. The smooth slopes of Moelfre are up on your left.*

2 After about ½ mile go through another gate and join a rough-surfaced wide track. Go LEFT along it. *The wild landscape of the Ysgethin valley is soon in full view. On your right, the rocky spur jutting out into the valley floor from the slopes of Moelfre is topped at the end by Craig y Dinas, a prehistoric small defensive enclosure. Further on, after going beyond the top of the spur, the parapets of the 17th or 18th century bridge, Pont Scethin, down on your right, will just be seen. On your left, the ruins just beyond the conifer trees are of a coaching inn, a reminder that the old coach road between Harlech and Bontddu crossed this valley, there being no possible route then via Barmouth. That route was not carved out of rock until 1798.* Stay along this rough surfaced track. Nearly ¾ mile past the end of the conifer trees, and clear of the last of the outcropping of rocks on the steep lower slopes of Moelfre on the left, you reach a position on the track which is nearly level with the lowest section of the grassy, gentler, ridge of moorland up on the left. Leave the track at this point and go LEFT over rough grass up towards the ridge. *When about half-way up, there is a fine last sweeping view back of the whole length of the Ysgethin valley.*

3 Near the top of the ridge, if you come to a vehicular grass track across your route, go LEFT along it, and bearing RIGHT where it forks very near the top, to reach a gate. If you miss this track, keep on going up and at the top of the ridge, look left for the wall coming down steeply from the summit of Moelfre. Go towards the point where it starts to level out and to the gate. soon seen in the wall. Go through and follow the path ahead and down, through a gap in the next wall, and on through another in the following wall. *The views now far ahead are across Tremadog Bay to the Lleyn Peninsula, while close ahead is Cwm Nantcol and, half-right, the rocky mass of Rhinog Fawr. Soon, more spectacular views open up to the right, revealing Rhinog Fach and the pass Bwlch Drws-Ardudwy between Fawr and Fach, and also the grassy top of Y Llethr, at 2475 feet the highest of the Rhinog range.* Continue down, through a third wall gap and over a stile at the next wall. From here the track goes half-LEFT, then RIGHT, alongside an old low wall and down to the valley road.

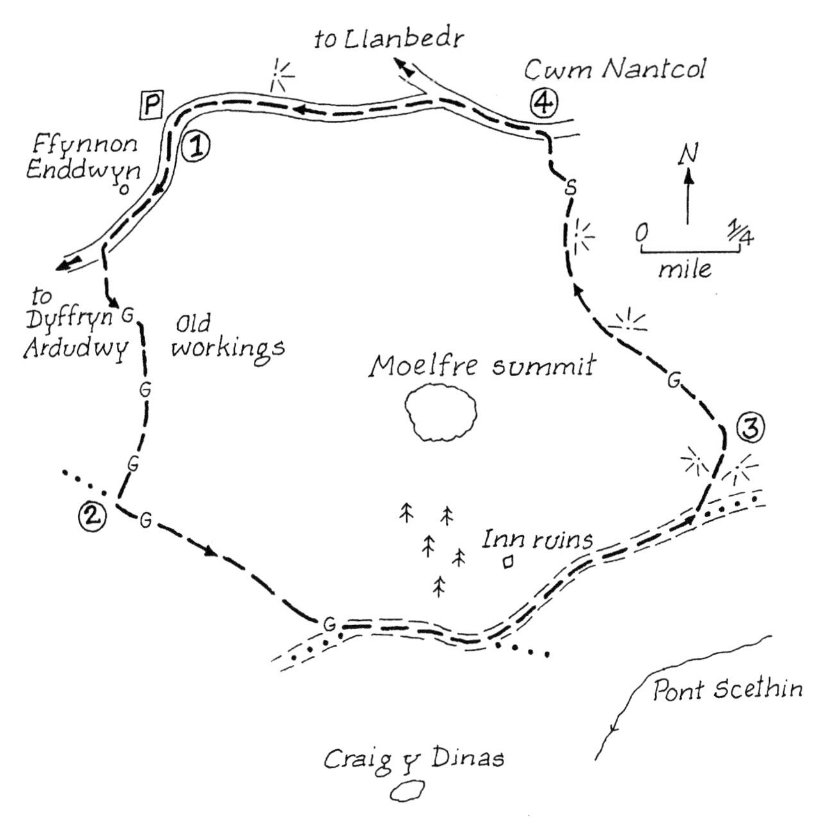

4 At the road go LEFT, and in ¼ mile LEFT again at the next road junction (signed Dyffryn Ardudwy). This quiet road takes you back to the start. *Enjoy the fine views back (east) up Cwm Nantcol. Opposite, across the valley (north), can be seen the hillsides of Walk* **14**.

Pont Scethin

PRONUNCIATION

These basic points should help non-Welsh speakers

Welsh	English equivalent
c	always hard, as in **c**at
ch	as in the Scottish word lo**ch**
dd	as th in **th**en
f	as **f** in of
ff	as **ff** in off
g	always hard as in got
ll	no real equivalent. It is like 'th' in **th**en, but with an 'L' sound added to it, giving '**thlan**' for the pronunciation of the Welsh 'Llan'.

In Welsh the accent usually falls on the last-but-one syllable of a word.

KEY TO THE MAPS

- Walk route and direction
- Metalled road
- Unsurfaced road
- Footpath/route adjoining walk route
- River/stream
- Trees
- Railway
- G Gate
- S Stile
- F.B. Footbridge
- Viewpoint
- P Parking
- T Telephone

THE COUNTRY CODE

- Be safe – plan ahead and follow any signs
- Leave gates and property as you find them
- Protect plants and animals, and take your litter home
- Keep dogs under close control
- Consider other people

The CroW Act 2000, implemented throughout Wales in May 2005, introduced new legal rights of access for walkers to designated open country, predominantly mountain, moor, heath or down, plus all registered common land. This access can be subject to restrictions and closure for land management or safety reasons for up to 28 days a year.

Published by
Kittiwake
3 Glantwymyn Village Workshops, Glantwymyn,
Machynlleth, Montgomeryshire SY20 8LY

First edition 2004. Minor revisions 2005. Reprinted 2007 & 2008 (twice).
New edition 2009.

We would like to thank the Wales Tourist Board for allowing us to use the main cover photograph.

Cover picture: Harlech Castle ©WTB 2004.

Printed by: MWL, Pontypool.

ISBN: **978 1 902302 68 3**